# Coors®*
# Taste of the West

*Pictured on the cover is Tacos al Carbon.
The recipe is on page 32.*

This seal assures you that every recipe in *Coors Taste of the West* has been tested in the Better Homes and Gardens® Test Kitchen. This means that each recipe is practical and reliable, and meets our high standards of taste appeal.

**Editor:** Anita Krajeski
**Project Editors:** Sandra Day, Pat Teberg   **Designers:** Deetra Leech, Stephen Lueder
**Contributing Editors:** Sam Arnold, Cinde Dolphin, Mary Louise McCullough, Charles Russell, Mike Wood

*Registered trademark of Adolph Coors Company.

Produced by Meredith Publishing Services, Locust at 17th, Des Moines, IA 50336
©Meredith Corporation, 1981. Second Edition, 1985. All Rights Reserved. Printed in U.S.A.

# Contents

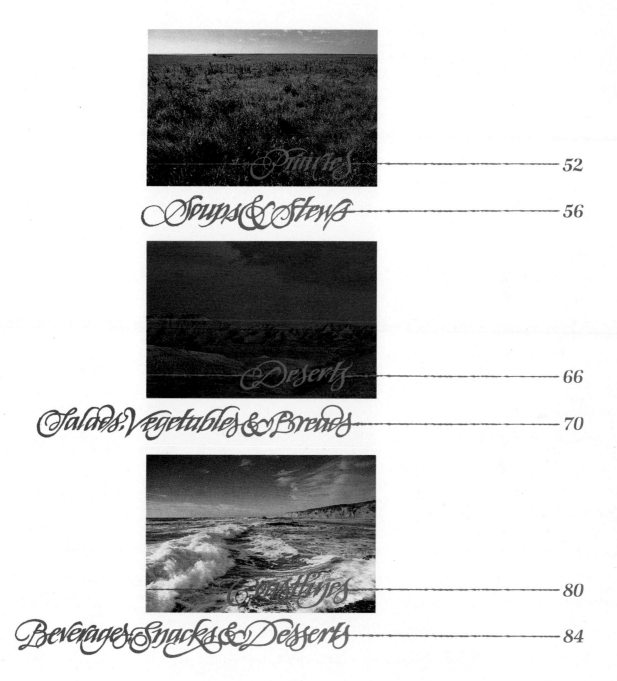

ADOLPH COORS

GOLDEN, COLORADO.

TRADE MARK

16TH AND WEWATTA STS
OPPOSITE
UNION DEPOT
DENVER.

## Settling the West

The story of the settlement of the American West is as vast in scope and full in detail as the mountains, deserts, prairies, rivers and coastlines where it unfolded. It is a story of romance and tragedy, freedom and conflict with characters as different as the adventurous Father Juniperro Serra and the colorful Buffalo Bill. Life in the early West was invigorating to some, treacherous to others. Indians, Spaniards, Mexicans and mountain men struggled alongside cowboys, pioneer women and gunfighters to carve out the legends we know today. Scandinavian and German farm families put their plows to the endless sea of grass, fighting locusts, hail and drought to create a granary for the world. Greek and Italian fishermen brought their families and traditions around Cape Horn to harvest the Pacific Ocean's vast quantities of fish. And Irish and Chinese laborers gandy danced their ribbon of steel to join the continent forever.

The cultures of the four continents which came together in this western frontier survived by adapting, and by adapting they added a new chapter to the history and heritage of American cooking. These settlers brought with them food preferences, old recipes and time-honored ways of cooking. Often these preferences differed from what the land had to offer; recipes and methods were changed accordingly. Strange new game such as buffalo, antelope and wild turkey tested a cook's resourcefulness. Campfires replaced stoves and ovens for cooking. Utensils, herbs and spices were limited.

For folks such as miners and cowboys, life often revolved around a working camp where a good cook was worth his weight in gold. Camps frequently were known for the skill of their cooks who could fashion delicious meals out of a minimum of supplies. On the farm, a family and its hired hands depended on a woman's cooking ability to provide them with nourishment and strength for their arduous chores. They ate hearty food grown on their farmlands. They drank milk fresh from their dairy animals, water from their wells, beer brewed in their newfound hometowns — and they cooked with all three.

These western settlers, sodbusters and gold seekers found imaginative ways to cook the natural plants and wildlife of their regions — their only food. By modifying old recipes and adapting some of the traditional foods of their countrymen, they created several of the dishes of the West.

This cook book is a result of their labors and the work of their grandchildren and great-grandchildren who adapted these recipes to fit their lifestyles and modern ingredients. In this book are dishes that have been passed through generations of pioneer families or survived by word of mouth for their novelty or good flavor. Like the people who settled the West, these dishes are not fancy. But they are sure to warm the soul and please the palate.

## The Coors Heritage

While these recipes were being created from pioneer life, one immigrant was working his way slowly across the United States to Golden, Colorado, where he would build a brewery that would grow up with the West.

Adolph Herman Joseph Coors, founder of Adolph Coors Company, was 21 when he left Rhenish Prussia (northwestern Germany) in 1868 and stowed away on a ship bound for Baltimore. An accomplished brewer, he had apprenticed at Henry Wenger's brewery in Dortmund and also worked at breweries in Kassel, Berlin and Uelzen. He left his native land as did many youths of his time, feeling oppressed by the militaristic Prussian environment. He was 25 when he reached Denver in 1872 and bought a partnership in a bottling firm with money he had earned at breweries in New York and Naperville, Illinois.

In Denver, Coors soon bought out his partner in the wine and beer bottling company and then met up with Jacob Schueler. Records indicate the two men were a study in opposites: Coors the stern, serious young man and Schueler the cane-toting *bon vivant*. With Schueler providing most of the capital, they set up a brewery in

# DINNER AT THE RESIDENCE

Dinner at the Coors residence, where Golden children peeked through the white picket fence "to see the Coors," was formal and not the place for children's tricks. Promptly at 6:25 every evening, Adolph Coors, Sr., reached for his pocket watch as he stood by the living room fireplace and called, "All ready?"

Hands washed, hair combed, the six children tumbled out of their rooms and fell into line behind their father and mother, whom they followed to the dining room "like little ducks," according to longtime housekeeper Alma Brushwiller.

The menu, planned every morning by Mrs. Coors, was usually soup or bouillon, meat, potato and vegetable served on warmed plates, a salad, and pies, cakes or cheesecakes for dessert. Meals were served on tables covered with white linen cloths stitched from the fine linen bags in which hops were shipped from Germany to the brewery.

Bill Coors, Chairman of the Board of Adolph Coors Company today, remembers his grandfather as a strict, stern, kind and gentle man. "When you grow up in a German family of that nature, where there's absolutely no tolerance for error, you're in a perpetual state of fear, or you turn into a perpetual rebel like my brothers and I did," he recalls, laughing.

Golden on the site of an old tannery where Coors had found his own gold — Pure Rocky Mountain Spring Water.

The brew that would refresh and quench the thirst of many a pioneer was first sold in 1874 with Coors himself behind the wheelbarrow that lugged 31-gallon oaken barrels through town. That first year Coors brewed 10 barrels a day, compared to more than 14 million barrels per year today. Coors beer reached nearby towns such as Denver and Blackhawk by horse and wagon. Fathers who lived near town got their supplies of beer for supper by sending their young sons to the saloon carrying tin buckets rimmed with lard which the bartender would fill. The lard prevented a head from forming on the beer, keeping the bartender from cheating the family out of a full bucket and also keeping the beer from foaming on the bumpy walk home. This old custom was called "rushing the growler."

Within a year the local *Colorado Transcript* newspaper applauded the brewery as having "leaped to the front rank of brewers in a remarkably short time." In 1880, Coors bought out Schueler, who wanted to spend more time on his other business investments. The next 39 years were years of prosperity and growth for Coors and his brewery — years that would long be remembered after his and other breweries were brought to their knees by Prohibition.

## Food and Beer

Most beer drinking in the late 19th Century was done at saloons; as much as 80 percent of Coors beer was sold in wooden kegs. The saloons were the town gathering place — for men only — and patrons bellied up to the brass railer bar to drink beer and eat the "free lunch." Saloons were required to sell food with beer, and in the days before inflation that meant much more than pretzels. Old-timers sampled everything from home-baked bread and pies to salami, pepperoni and cheese.

The saloon wasn't the only place where beer figured prominently with food. Louisa Weber, who married Coors in 1879, fed her husband's brewery workers daily for years at her home on the brewery grounds. She is said to have cooked simple meals of meat and potatoes with homemade bread and gravy. Often her husband's brew came in handy as a marinade for sauerbraten or ribs. This tradition of preparing simple but delicious meals lives today in the weekly luncheons at the original Coors residence on the brewery grounds where the Coors family hosts community leaders from Colorado.

Even before his marriage to Louisa Weber, Coors built his own version of the traditional German beer gardens next to the house. It became a favorite pastime of his Denver acquaintances to take an open-air streetcar from Denver to Golden for a picnic. They would spend a day at the beer garden, eating, drinking from barrels of cold beer and sunning. Coors entertained as many as 800 people at one time at the beer garden. In winter, a nearby pond on the brewery grounds was a local skating spot which Coors kept brushed and well-lit for public skating.

**The Dry Years**

But the popularity of the golden brew that the local residents enjoyed so much meant nothing to the churning wave of Prohibitionist fever which swept the country in the early 20th Century and shut down Colorado's brewers in 1914.

By the time Prohibition became law Adolph Coors, Sr., had amassed a fortune of about $2 million. He could have chosen to close his brewery and live a comfortable, retired life and provide for his family. Instead, he vowed to keep the doors of his business open and as many employees on the payroll as possible. To do this, records show that Adolph Coors cut his salary and the salaries of the members of his family employed at the brewery. But these cost-cutting measures alone were hardly adequate to meet the challenge of a dry land. And so Adolph Coors developed malted milk, near beer and ceramic businesses in hopes of sustaining the life of his company.

Coors became a leading producer of malted milk, selling his products throughout

# BUCKSKIN PARTIES

In the early 1930s, the late Adolph Coors, Jr., son of the company's founder, would take a group of employees hunting to provide venison for the annual brewery buckskin parties. After days of hunting, the men returned to Golden, leaving elk, deer or bear at the local mercantile butcher for dressing. The Coors family cook then spent nearly a week preparing roasts and refrigerating them in the huge eight-compartment refrigerator at the Coors mansion on the brewery grounds. The day before the feast, which was held on Sunday afternoon, the cook and her assistant spent all day and night finishing roasts, grinding meat for meat loaves and marinating some cuts in vinegar or Coors beer with bay leaves, cloves and peppercorns.

They used only "Old Betsy," a wood and coal stove with three ovens and eight burner lids. That one stove was used to cook all the meat for as many as 1,500 guests — including brewery employees, their families and invited public officials. Meat was served with cheese and rye bread sliced "tissue paper thin," a preference of Adolph Coors, Jr., and, of course, accompanied by mugs of Coors beer.

# THE PUREST BEER IN AMERICA

Coors beer is brewed, purified and distributed under the most exacting standards in the industry, guaranteeing the consumer a beer unparalleled in quality, purity, freshness and flavor. Absolutely no artificial ingredients, nitrosamines, chemicals or additives are ever used or found in Coors beer, allowing Coors to say: "We make the purest beer in America."

Coors uses four all-natural ingredients blended in a six-step brewing process — one of the longest and most sophisticated in the brewing industry — to attain the distinctive taste and quality of its beer.

Premium barleys, developed by Coors agronomists, are roasted into malt to give Coors beer its rich taste and golden color. Hops from Germany and the Pacific Northwest provide Coors' characteristic flavor, bitterness and aroma. Rice and other cereals give the beer its light body. Pure Rocky Mountain Spring Water is used in its natural form to bring out the distinctive flavor of Coors.

Brewing Coors begins with the malting process. Premium barley is moistened and allowed to sprout and is then carefully dried, roasted and aged.

In the next step, precise amounts of malt, rice and other cereals are combined with Pure Rocky Mountain Spring water in large, clean copper kettles and are heated to convert malt, rice and other cereal starches to sugars. Liquid extract from the malt and cereals is then boiled with special imported and domestic hops. The resulting rich liquid, called wort, is cooled and sent to the fermenting cellar.

In the fermenting cellar, the wort is mixed with yeast and is placed in fermenting tanks. Under carefully controlled time and temperature conditions, the yeast works on the sugars in the wort to produce alcohol and carbon dioxide, turning the mixture into Coors beer.

After fermentation, the beer is allowed to age in glass-lined tanks for an average of 45 days, one of the longest aging periods in the brewing industry. Once aged, the beer is ready for the finishing process where its alcohol and carbonation levels are standardized.

Coors is brewed as pure as beer can be in virtually sterile conditions. As a result, Coors — unlike other brewers — does not have to pasteurize its beer to achieve biological purity. The unique Coors sterile fill process means that from brewing to packaging, Coors is handled in a bacteria-free environment. No other brewer in the world duplicates this process.

Finally, Coors beers are triple-filtered and packaged. Realizing that time, heat and light are enemies of beer flavor, Coors brewers have worked to eliminate these factors. Coors packages its beer in dark bottles and cans and encourages retailers to keep it refrigerated. Although Coors beer will not spoil in unrefrigerated conditions, it, like any other beer, tastes best when it's kept cold.

Coors also maintains tight inventory controls on distribution and retailers to ensure fast turnover of Coors beer in the marketplace. Distributors are required to remove from retailers' stocks any beer more than two months away from the brewery and to replace it with fresh beer.

Coors' uncompromising dedication to quality, regardless of expense or time involved, truly results in the purest beer in America.

the western states to soda fountains. And national candy companies bought Coors malted milk for use as an ingredient in candy bars.

Adolph Coors Company also ran a ceramics plant which produced chemical and scientific porcelain, dinnerware and flame-resistant cooking utensils throughout Prohibition. Since World War II, the company has become the leading international producer of highly technical industrial ceramics and is now known as the Coors Porcelain Company.

Besides malted milk and ceramics, Coors also produced near beer, a nonalcoholic beer substitute brewed like regular beer — but with the alcohol distilled out. Unlike bathtub gin, which gained popularity as the cocktail party drink of the era, near beer failed to win over the drinking public.

But the production of near beer was not without its blessings. Since near beer was produced throughout the dry years, Coors was able to produce its beer again immediately when Prohibition ended in 1933.

Adolph Coors died in 1929 — four years before the end of Prohibition. In an effort to keep his company alive, he had expended his entire fortune, never considering that the controversial law which marred his dream would one day be repealed. But Adolph Coors' company — and his beer — survived.

In Golden on the first "wet" day, appropriately it was raining. But the brewery grounds were crowded as people came by truck, car, bicycle and on foot — carrying buckets, bottles, bowls and tubs — to get their first real Coors beer in two decades.

Of the 750 breweries which reopened in 1933, fewer than 30 remain today. The brewing industry has followed the West's growth, spreading out and becoming increasingly competitive. Today, Coors is the largest single brewery in the country, with 20 subsidiary operations and four brands of beer. Coors Premium, Herman Joseph's 1868, Coors Light and George Killian's Irish Red are among the products brewed in Golden on the site of Adolph's original brewery.

## Man's Oldest Beverage

The story of the West and the story of Coors span four generations, and there are Coors employees whose family history covers all four of those generations. Today, grandsons and great-grandsons of the founder operate the world's single largest brewery. But the story doesn't end there. Coors is continuing to move production and sales east.

Still, the story of Coors remains part of the West. Coors was in those western kitchens long before this cookbook was compiled, just as home brewing was known long before recorded history. The first known recipe for grain fermentation dates back to the 7th Century B.C., and women in ancient times made

their brews by mashing baked bread with water.

Early Mayflower shipboard records show that the first Pilgrims landed at Plymouth Rock because they had run out of supplies or, as one passenger explained in his diary, "Our victuals being much spent, especially our beere …" Records from colonial, Revolutionary and pioneer days show that cooking with beer was popular for the distinct flavor it imparted to foods.

What women discovered in their kitchens years ago remains true today: Beer has unique effects on food. It can be mixed as a flavor or spice, added to batters to lighten cakes and pancakes, or used as a marinade for fish, poultry and meat. Alcohol in beer evaporates when food is cooked, leaving a subtle and distinctive flavor which can't be matched or bought in a spice can.

The recipes in this book use beer, are good to eat with beer, or stand alone as recipes of that western heritage that made America and Coors what we know today. It is a heritage rich with pride, formed by the pioneer spirit. It is the food of the good life, the life of the West.

*Mountains*

For early American settlers hungering to make their fortunes, the mountains were the great western land barrier to conquer. First came Spanish Conquistadores followed by fur trappers, each learning new methods of survival in the Rockies, Sierra Nevadas and Cascades.

Next came the gold rush miners, bringing a diversity of ethnic backgrounds to the rugged elegance of the mountains. Finally, homesteaders and their families settled the valleys and basins to farm. The permanence of civilization set in, and the traditions of the mountains were born.

## Western Trappers

Long-haired trappers in buckskin pants prowled the mountains for fur-bearing animals, whose skins they sold for profit, and opened the door to the trailblazers who followed. Trappers survived by eating what they could catch or kill. Often it was rattlesnake meat and beaver tail for dinner. Buffalo, however, was the favorite food of trappers and other settlers.

The buffalo had a mystique that captured the attention of the early western settlers. Meriwether Lewis wrote of the "tremendous roaring" of buffalo bulls near Great Falls, Montana, and that he "ate of the small guts of the buffalo, cooked over a blazing fire in the Indian stile [sic] without any preparation or washing or other cleansing and found them very good."

One pioneer woman said buffalo soup was better than soups from the best hotels in New York and Philadelphia. She compared buffalo marrow to the most luscious butters and oils. Buffalo tongues were often shipped East where they became a delicacy served in restaurants and were among the most expensive items on the menu.

Buffalo hunters could make up to 30 cents apiece for each tongue, while hides brought from $1.50 to $2 at Kansas hide depots.

The Santa Fe Railroad tie to Fort Dodge, Kansas, was finished in 1872, linking the fur country with the East. During the next three years, 400,000 buffalo hides were shipped annually. But the nation's voracious appetite for buffalo hides and meat meant that the animals' days were numbered. Dwindling herds meant that the last large buffalo hunt was held in 1883.

Often, buffalo hunters would return to St. Louis and other towns after a hunt, full of tales of life on the trail. Some had married Indian women and developed a taste for native dishes, and they no doubt passed along descriptions of this food, encouraging others to try Indian cooking techniques. Dried foods, such as jerky and pemmican, developed centuries before by the Indians, became popular trail foods of the mountain men, and later, the settlers.

## Gold and Silver Miners

Before the trappers and hunters depleted the natural fur supply, miners came to the mountains. Early mining camps in California, Montana, Colorado, Idaho and Wyoming were populated with Chinese, Blacks, Spaniards, Germans, French and Scotch-Irish, among others, all struggling to make their fortunes in gold or silver. They pitched tents, built dugouts and lived off wild game such as bear, elk, moose and birds.

Slowly, more families joined the men in their search for gold, often moving in small groups. Montana miner Granville Stuart described the arrival of the first woman in his mining camp in 1862, "Every man in camp has shaved and changed his shirt since this family arrived."

Mountain settlers from the East and West arrived in an assortment of ways. Some came by foot, pushing handcarts, some by open horse-drawn wagon, and some by foot, carrying a bag of belongings with flour and a slab of bacon. Along the mountain trails they found tent saloons and lean-to taverns where they could quench their thirst with a warm brew. Necessities such as grain and mining tools were often shipped in shallow-draft, wood-burning steamboats up the rivers from cities such as St. Louis to towns where they were taken by wagon train to mining outposts.

Miners' families often traded recipes and blended their traditions, using the few ingredients

# INDEPENDENCE ROCK

One of the lasting remnants of hearty western trailblazers is Independence Rock in what is now central Wyoming. It was the gateway to the mountains for settlers and miners, many from Missouri who were two months into their journey. They stopped here at the foot of the mountains to celebrate and relax before beginning the climb.

Small bands would stretch like a string of tiny lights at night with campfires glowing while strangers danced and sang together, sharing their food and drink. On July 4, 1847, a pioneer wrote that 1,000 people congregated at the rock near the Sweetwater Stream with the Wind River Mountains to the west. The families contributed to a huge feast of cakes, pickles, dried beef and preserves, rice pudding, beans, dried fruit and savory pie made of sage hen and rabbit with gravy.

They must have known they were part of a great destiny, for hundreds carved their names in the huge granite rock before moving on. Today, Independence Rock still bears the names of some of those travelers, carvings that have withstood the winds, rains and hail where the mountains meet the plains.

they had, making do with few frills. To remove the wild game taste of some animals, the miners' wives often soaked meat overnight in salt water or — if it was tough — soaked it in vinegar, water or beer for a few days. Some canned food in tins called "airtights" was available in the camps, but diets had to be simple and nourishing.

Colorado history shows that Cornish miners from England brought many colorful traditions that were adopted by their neighbors. Called "Cousin Jacks," partly due to their family loyalty, they provided the Cornish "pasty," a substantial meal that a miner could carry into a deep shaft. Pasties were a mixture of meat and vegetables enclosed in a crimped pastry crust, similiar to a turnover. Today, the pasty is still available in restaurants in Golden, Colorado, where many Cornish families lived and worked at the Coors brewery.

The gold rush in Colorado began in 1859, the same year that the first swig of beer became available in the area. By the 1880s, breweries numbered 23 in Colorado, including Golden's own Coors brewery. At one point there was a brewery in nearly every Colorado mining town. The brewery often served as the local post office and general store as well. These towns also had several saloons where the early trailblazers would come to enjoy conversation, drink beer and risk their hard-earned gold dust in games of chance.

# FOOD ON THE DRIVE

The chuck wagon was a place to congregate on the roundup or trail drive. The cook — always reputed to be mean and cantankerous — reigned supreme.

No man raised dust near the domain of the cook and his wagon. Likewise, no man would help himself to any provisions from the chuck wagon.

The back of the wagon was fitted with drawers and shelves to carry utensils and supplies. A "cooney" or cradle-like device under the bed of the wagon carried wood or cow chips for fuel.

A jug for the sourdough, a sack of flour, cans of coffee, a supply of salt, potatoes, canned tomatoes, sugar, molasses, lard, salt pork and beans were standard supplies. All the cooking and eating utensils had to be carried as well.

*Trail-driven cattle of the Old West were tougher than today's beef, and the meat often had to be tenderized. Chicken Fried Steak became a very popular way to prepare the somewhat tough round steak, and is still a favorite in Texas. The faster you cook it, the juicier it will be.*

## CHICKEN FRIED STEAK

1½   pounds beef top round steak, cut ½ inch thick
¾   cup all-purpose flour
½   teaspoon salt
⅛   teaspoon pepper
¼   cup *Coors* beer
¼   cup cooking oil
2   tablespoons all-purpose flour
1   cup milk
½   cup *Coors* beer

Cut meat into 6 portions. Pound steak between two pieces of waxed paper till ¼ inch thick. Stir together the ¾ cup flour, the salt and pepper. Dip each piece of meat into flour mixture, then into the ¼ cup Coors, then into the flour mixture again. In 12-inch skillet brown meat in hot oil, turning once (about 3 to 4 minutes per side). Remove meat to platter; keep warm. Blend the 2 tablespoons flour into drippings in skillet. Stir in milk, then the ½ cup Coors. Cook and

stir till thickened and bubbly.
Cook and stir 1 to 2 minutes
more. Pass sauce with meat.
Makes 6 servings.

## RANCH TOAST AND HAM
*(pictured right)*

  1  **fully-cooked ham
center slice, cut 1
inch thick (about
2½ pounds)**
  2  **tablespoons cooking
oil**
  ½  **cup all-purpose flour**
  1  **tablespoon sugar**
  1  **teaspoon baking soda**
  1  **cup buttermilk**
  2  **eggs**
  6  **1-inch-thick slices
bread
Shortening or
cooking oil for
shallow frying
Maple-flavored syrup
or molasses**

In large heavy skillet cook ham
slice in the 2 tablespoons hot
cooking oil over medium heat for
16 to 18 minutes total time,
turning meat occasionally.
Transfer to platter; keep warm.
In mixing bowl, stir together
flour, sugar and soda. Add
buttermilk and eggs; beat
smooth with rotary beater. Dip
bread into batter; let stand 1
minute on each side. Fry in
8-inch skillet in ¼ inch hot
shortening about 1 minute per
side or till crisp and golden.
Serve batter-fried bread with
slices of ham; pass syrup to
drizzle over. Makes 6 servings.

Ranch Toast and Ham

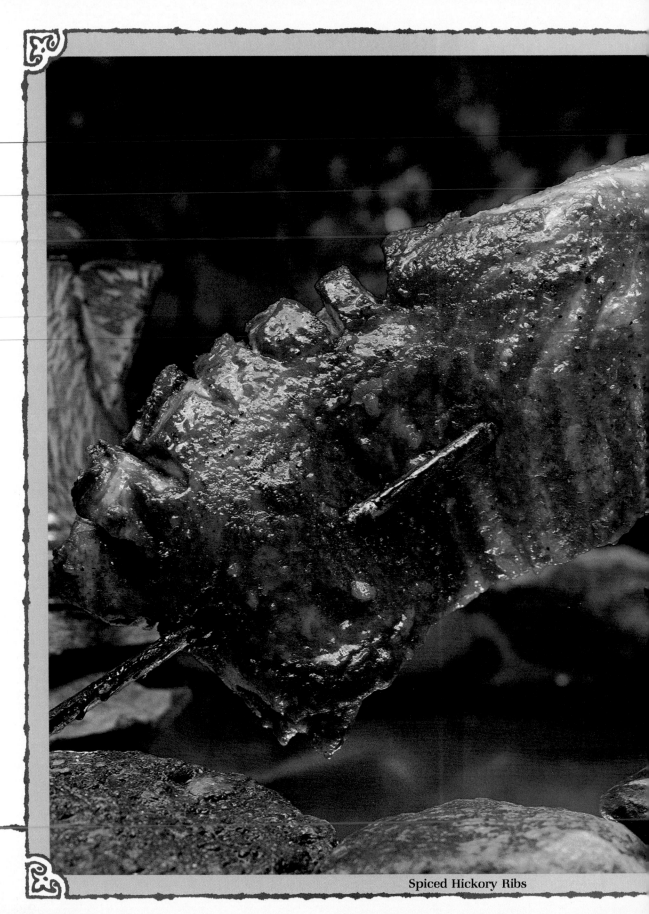

Spiced Hickory Ribs

## SPICED HICKORY RIBS
*(pictured left)*

- 1½ teaspoons ground ginger
- 1½ teaspoons ground coriander
- ½ teaspoon paprika
- 4 pounds pork loin back ribs or spareribs
  Hickory chips
- ½ cup peach preserves
- ½ cup *Coors* beer

Combine ginger, coriander, paprika, 1 teaspoon *salt* and ¼ teaspoon *pepper;* rub onto meaty side of ribs. Cover and chill 2 hours. About an hour before cooking time, soak hickory chips in water to cover. Lace ribs accordion-style on spit rod; secure with holding forks. Arrange hot coals on both sides of shallow foil drip pan. Drain hickory chips; sprinkle some over coals. Attach spit; position drip pan under meat. Turn on rotisserie; lower hood. Grill ribs over medium coals 1 hour or till done. Sprinkle coals with chips every 20 minutes. In blender container combine preserves and Coors; cover and blend till smooth. Brush mixture onto ribs during last 10 minutes of grilling. Heat and pass remaining glaze. Makes 4 servings.

 *Beer often is used in game recipes to tenderize meat and add flavor. It also helps remove the "gamey" taste often found in venison.*

## STUFFED VENISON STEAKS

- 2 pounds venison or beef steak, cut ¾ inch thick
- 2½ cups *Coors* beer
- ⅓ cup cooking oil
  • • •
- 8 slices bacon
- ½ cup sliced green onion
- ½ cup dairy sour cream
- ¼ cup all-purpose flour
  Dash paprika

Cut venison into 6 pieces. Cut a pocket into one side of each piece of meat. Place meat in plastic bag; set in shallow pan. Pour *1½ cups* of the Coors over meat in bag; add oil and close bag. Chill overnight, turning meat several times. Drain meat; discard marinade. Pat meat dry. Cook bacon till crisp. Drain, reserving 2 tablespoons drippings. Crumble bacon; combine with onion. Stuff mixture into pockets in meat. Brown steaks on both sides in reserved drippings. Sprinkle with *salt* and *pepper;* add ¾ *cup* of the Coors to skillet. Cover and simmer over low heat for 45 to 60 minutes or till venison is tender. Remove meat to platter. Measure pan juices; add enough water to make 1½ cups liquid. Stir together sour cream, flour, and the remaining ¼ cup Coors. Stir some of the pan juices into sour cream mixture; return all to pan. Cook and stir till thickened and bubbly. Cook and stir 1 minute more. Season to taste with a little *salt* and *pepper.* Sprinkle with paprika. Serves 6.

*Sauerbraten marinated in beer was originally prepared by Louisa Coors in the late 1800s and is still a family favorite.*

## MRS. COORS' SAUERBRATEN

- 1 12-ounce can *Coors* beer
- 1½ cups red wine vinegar
- 2 medium onions, sliced
- 1 lemon, sliced
- 12 whole cloves
- 6 whole black peppercorns, crushed
- 4 bay leaves, crushed
- 1 tablespoon sugar
- ¼ teaspoon ground ginger
- 1 4-pound boneless beef rump roast
- 2 tablespoons cooking oil
- ½ cup chopped onion
- ½ cup chopped carrot
- ¼ cup chopped celery
- 1 cup broken gingersnaps
  Hot buttered noodles

Combine first nine ingredients and 1 tablespoon *salt*. Place meat in plastic bag; set in shallow pan. Pour marinade over meat; close bag. Refrigerate 72 hours, turning occasionally. Remove meat; pat dry. Strain marinade; set aside. Brown meat in hot oil. Drain off fat. Add reserved marinade, chopped onion, carrot and celery. Cover; simmer 2 hours or till meat is tender. Remove meat. Reserve 2 cups of the cooking liquid and vegetables. Stir in gingersnaps and ⅔ cup *water*. Cook and stir till thickened. Serve with meat and noodles. Makes 12 servings.

## WILD DUCK AND MUSHROOMS

- 2 1½- to 2-pound ready-to-cook wild ducks, quartered
- 4 tablespoons butter
- 1 12-ounce can *Coors* beer
- 1 cup small, whole fresh mushrooms
- ¼ cup sliced green onion
- 2 bay leaves
- 2 tablespoons cornstarch
  Snipped parsley
  Hot cooked wild rice

In Dutch oven brown duck pieces in *2 tablespoons* of the butter. Drain off excess fat. Stir in Coors, mushrooms, green onion, bay leaves, ½ teaspoon *salt* and a dash *pepper*. Cover and simmer, over low heat, 1¼ to 1½ hours or till duck is tender. Remove duck. Discard bay leaves. Measure pan juices; add additional Coors, if necessary, to measure 2 cups liquid. In saucepan melt the remaining 2 tablespoons butter; stir in cornstarch. Stir in pan juices. Cook and stir till thickened. Cook and stir 1 to 2 minutes more. Spoon some of sauce over duck; sprinkle with parsley. Pass remaining sauce. Serve with wild rice. Serves 4.

## PHEASANT WITH SAUSAGE STUFFING

- ¼ pound bulk pork sausage
- ½ cup chopped apple
- ½ cup chopped celery
- ¼ cup chopped onion
- 2 cups dry bread cubes
- 2 tablespoons snipped parsley
- ¼ teaspoon dried thyme, crushed
- ¼ teaspoon dried marjoram, crushed
- 2 to 3 tablespoons *Coors* beer
  • • •
- 2 2-to-3 pound pheasants
- ¼ cup bacon drippings
- ¼ cup *Coors*

In skillet cook sausage, apple, celery and onion till sausage is browned and vegetables are tender; drain well. Stir together sausage mixture, bread cubes, parsley, thyme, marjoram and a dash *pepper*. Add the 2 to 3 tablespoons Coors, tossing lightly. Sprinkle cavities of pheasants with a little *salt*. Stuff lightly with sausage mixture. Place birds, breast side up, on rack in shallow roasting pan. Tie wings to body; tie legs together. (Or, quarter birds. In baking pan, shape stuffing into 8 mounds. Place a pheasant quarter atop each stuffing mound.) Combine bacon drippings and the remaining ¼ cup Coors. Roast birds, uncovered, in 350° oven for 1½ to 2 hours or till tender, brushing occasionally with dripping mixture. Makes 4 to 6 servings.

# AUTHENTIC TEXAS BARBECUE

The experts agree on one thing about Texas barbecue: the slower you cook it, the better. But the meat that is used is open to discussion. Brisket and ribs are the most popular, but smoked sausage, chicken, and cabrito (young goat) are also common. The rule is, there must be plenty of accompaniments: boiled pinto beans, potatoes or potato salad, cole slaw, corn bread or biscuits, pickled peppers, watermelon and ice cream.

The secret to that real Texas barbecue flavor is in the wood chips that go on the coals—they produce the smoke that gives the barbecue its distinctive flavor. Mesquite chips are the best, but hickory or pecan chips are also quite good.

The barbecue sauce should be a dark brick-red color, and thick. It should be spicy, and a little sweet. The sauce is basted on the meat while it cooks, but you should save some to use as a soppin' sauce when you eat it. If it isn't messy, it isn't barbecue!

## TEXAS BRISKET BARBECUE

- 1 12-ounce can *Coors* beer
- ½ cup tomato juice
- ½ cup chopped onion
- 1 clove garlic, minced
- ¼ cup Worcestershire sauce
- ¼ cup catsup
- 2 tablespoons brown sugar
- 1 lemon slice
- 1 tablespoon paprika
- 2 teaspoons dry mustard
- Several dashes bottled hot pepper sauce
- 3 to 4 cups mesquite or hickory chips
- 1 5- to 6-pound beef brisket

In 1½-quart saucepan combine Coors, tomato juice, onion, garlic, Worcestershire sauce, catsup, brown sugar, lemon, paprika, mustard, hot pepper sauce, 1 teaspoon *salt*, and ½ teaspoon *pepper*. Simmer, uncovered, for 30 minutes or till reduced to about 1½ cups.

About an hour before cooking time, soak mesquite or hickory chips in enough water to cover. In covered grill arrange hot coals on both sides of a foil drip pan. Drain chips. Sprinkle the coals with some of the chips. Place brisket atop grill over drip pan. Brush with some of the barbecue sauce. Lower hood or cover meat with foil tent; grill 1 hour, adding additional coals and chips as needed. Turn brisket, brushing both sides with additional sauce. Lower grill hood again; grill 50 to 55 minutes more or till meat is well done, adding more coals and chips as needed. Brush with sauce frequently during last 20 minutes of cooking. Heat and pass any remaining sauce, discarding lemon slice. Makes 12 to 16 servings.

*For Texas Barbecued Ribs:* For 4 pounds pork loin spareribs, use 2 cups mesquite or hickory chips. Grill as above except grill only 1 hour, turning once. Brush with sauce as above. Serves 4 to 6.

# RESPECTED HOSPITALITY

In Idaho, when a miner was away, he would leave his cabin open with food inside for anyone who needed it.

These trusting miners would even leave gold dust on the table of the vacant, open cabin.

Strangers often entered, ate, stayed the night and departed, grateful for the hospitality of food and drink.

But the stranger who helped himself to the gold dust was pursued, captured and promptly hanged.

## BRATWURST 'N' BEER

- 1 pound fresh bratwurst
- ½ cup chopped onion
- 2 tablespoons cooking oil
- ¾ cup beef broth
- ½ cup *Coors* beer
- 1 tablespoon brown sugar
- 2 bay leaves
- ¼ teaspoon dried thyme, crushed
- 2 tablespoons all-purpose flour
  Hot cooked noodles
- 2 tablespoons snipped parsley

In 10-inch skillet cook bratwurst and onion in oil over medium heat till bratwurst is brown and onion is tender.

Drain off fat. Add broth, Coors, sugar, bay leaves, thyme and ¼ teaspoon *pepper*. Bring to boiling; reduce heat. Simmer, covered, about 20 minutes or till done. Remove bratwurst; keep warm. Discard bay leaves. For sauce, blend ¼ cup *cold water* into flour; stir into hot beer mixture. Cook and stir till bubbly; cook and stir 2 minutes more. Pour over bratwurst and noodles. Top with parsley. Makes 4 servings.

## RABBIT IN MUSTARD SAUCE

*(pictured right)*

- ¼ cup all-purpose flour
- ¼ teaspoon ground nutmeg
- 1 1½- to 2-pound ready-to-cook rabbit, cut up
- 2 slices bacon
- 8 to 12 whole boiling onions
- 1 cup *Coors* beer
- 1 large bay leaf, crumbled
- 1 teaspoon instant chicken bouillon granules
- ¼ teaspoon dried thyme, crushed
- ½ cup light cream
- 2 egg yolks
- 1 tablespoon prepared mustard
- 2 tablespoons snipped parsley

Combine flour, nutmeg and a dash *pepper*; coat rabbit with mixture. In 10-inch skillet cook bacon till crisp; drain, reserving drippings in pan. Crumble bacon; set aside. Brown rabbit in reserved drippings about 5 minutes on each side. Add onions, Coors, bay leaf, bouillon granules, thyme and crumbled bacon. Cover and simmer 50 to 60 minutes or till meat is tender. Remove meat, onions and bacon to platter; keep warm. Strain pan juices; add water, if necessary, to measure ½ cup liquid. Pour juices into a small saucepan. Beat cream with egg yolks, mustard, ¼ teaspoon *salt* and a dash *pepper*; stir into pan juices. Cook and stir till thickened, but do not boil. Pour sauce over meat; sprinkle with parsley. Makes 4 servings.

## COORS BARBECUE SAUCE

- 1 cup catsup
- 1 cup *Coors* beer
- ½ cup chopped onion
- ¼ cup vinegar
- 1 tablespoon Worcestershire sauce
- 1 tablespoon prepared mustard
- ⅛ teaspoon bottled hot pepper sauce

Combine catsup, Coors, onion, vinegar, Worcestershire, mustard, pepper sauce and ½ teaspoon *salt*. Bring to boiling; reduce heat and simmer, uncovered, 30 minutes. Use to baste pork ribs, chops, steaks or burgers last 15 to 20 minutes of grilling. Pass remaining sauce. Makes 2 cups.

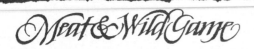

Rabbit in Mustard Sauce

**Chili Tostadas**

*Early settlers brought sheep West to provide meat and wool. Later, when the cattle industry began moving West, wars erupted between cattlemen and sheepmen over grazing lands. Cattlemen scornfully called sheep "woolies."*

## WOOLLIES IN BEER

4 **lamb shanks (3½ pounds)**
2 **tablespoons lard or cooking oil**
1 **12-ounce can Coors beer**
1 **cup finely chopped onion**
1 **cup finely chopped carrot**
1 **cup chopped celery**
1 **8-ounce can tomato sauce**
1 **clove garlic, minced**
1 **bay leaf**
½ **teaspoon salt**
⅛ **teaspoon pepper**
 **Hot cooked noodles**
 **Snipped parsley**

In Dutch oven brown lamb in hot melted lard or cooking oil; drain off excess fat. In mixing bowl stir together Coors, onion, carrot, celery, tomato sauce, garlic, bay leaf, salt and pepper. Pour over lamb. Cover; simmer for 1½ hours or till meat is tender.

Arrange lamb and vegetables atop hot cooked noodles on serving platter; keep warm. Remove bay leaf from tomato mixture; discard. Skim excess fat from sauce. Boil sauce,

# TOUGH TOWNS

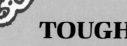

Western towns were built in a hurry. Dusty streets and wooden sidewalks, fronting one- and two-story wooden buildings, seemed to pop up almost overnight. Hotels, boardinghouses and saloons were frequented by hunters, trappers, prospectors, cowboys, stagecoach drivers, dance-hall girls, gamblers and gunmen.

In the 1860s, Julesburg, in north-eastern Colorado, became known as the toughest town on the 2,000-mile-long Overland Stage route. Even the stage company's superintendent, Joseph Slade, was notorious for his gun disputes and is credited with killing several men, including Julesburg's founder. Slade's idea of fun was to get drunk, ride his horse right into the saloons and shoot out the plate glass windows.

uncovered, till reduced to 1½ cups (about 5 to 7 minutes). Season to taste with salt and pepper. Spoon some of the sauce over lamb and noodles. Sprinkle with parsley. Pass remaining sauce. Serves 4 to 6.

## CHILI TOSTADAS

1 **pound ground beef**
½ **cup chopped onion**
1 **12-ounce can Coors beer**
1 **6-ounce can tomato paste**
1 **4-ounce can chopped green chilies**
1 **tablespoon chili powder**
½ **teaspoon sugar**
½ **teaspoon salt**
8 **6-inch corn tortillas Cooking oil**
1 **16-ounce can refried beans Shredded lettuce**
2 **tomatoes, chopped**
2 **cups shredded Monterey Jack cheese (8 ounces)**
1 **avocado, seeded, peeled and sliced**

In skillet cook ground beef and onion till meat is brown and onion is tender. Drain. Stir in Coors, tomato paste, green chilies, chili powder, sugar and salt; heat to boiling. Reduce heat; simmer, uncovered, for 20 minutes or till of desired consistency. Meanwhile, in small skillet cook tortillas, one at a time, in ½ inch hot oil for 20 to 40 seconds on each side or till crisp and golden. Drain on paper toweling. In small saucepan heat beans. To serve, place a tortilla on each plate; spread with beans. Spoon on meat sauce. Sprinkle with lettuce, tomatoes and cheese. Top with avocado slices. Makes 8 servings.

## RED FLANNEL HASH

- 1 large onion, chopped
- 1 tablespoon butter
  or margarine
- 1 pound ground chuck
- 3 medium beets, cooked,
  peeled, and diced
- 2 medium potatoes,
  cooked, peeled and
  diced
- 2 tablespoons light
  cream

In oven-going skillet cook onion in butter till tender. Combine *uncooked* meat, beets, potatoes and ½ teaspoon *pepper*; spread evenly in skillet. Cook over medium-low heat 20 minutes or till meat is cooked; stir occasionally. Spoon off fat. Drizzle cream over meat mixture. Transfer skillet to broiler. Broil 3 to 4 inches from heat 5 minutes or till crusty on top. Makes 6 servings.

## CHINESE RAILWAY WORKERS' BEEF CHOW MEIN

- 2 tablespoons
  cornstarch
- 2 teaspoons grated fresh
  gingerroot
- 1 teaspoon mustard seed
- 1 dried hot red chili
  pepper, crushed
  (½ teaspoon)
- 1 cup *Coors* beer
- ¼ cup bottled steak sauce
- 2 tablespoons soy sauce
- ½ pound long fettuccine-
  type Chinese noodles
- ½ cup cooking oil

- 2 medium yellow onions,
  cut into 1-inch
  wedges
- 6 bias-sliced green
  onions
- 2 cloves garlic, minced
- ¾ pound beef or buffalo
  sirloin, cut into thin
  strips
- 1 large green pepper, cut
  into 1x1½-inch
  strips
- 1 large sweet red
  pepper, cut into
  1x1½-inch strips
- 8 water chestnuts, sliced
- 2 dried mushrooms,
  soaked and sliced
- 2 cups fresh bean
  sprouts
- 1 cup bias-sliced celery
- 1 cup toasted broken
  walnuts
  Snipped parsley

In bowl combine first 4 ingredients. Stir in Coors, steak sauce and soy sauce; set aside. Cook noodles in large amount of boiling salted water 3 to 4 minutes or till tender. Drain; rinse with cold water. Drain well, gently wiping nearly dry with paper toweling; set aside.

In heavy 10-inch oven-going skillet heat 2 *tablespoons* of oil over medium heat. Add noodles; cook 4 to 5 minutes or till bottom of noodles is lightly browned. Loosen noodles and invert onto plate. Add another 2 *tablespoons* oil to skillet. Slide noodles back into pan, browned side up. Cook 4 to 5 minutes or till bottom of noodles is lightly browned.

Remove from heat; keep warm in 350° oven. In wok or large skillet heat 2 *tablespoons* oil over high heat. Add onions and garlic; cook and stir 1 minute. Remove onions and garlic; set aside. Heat remaining oil. Gradually add meat, stirring constantly. Add peppers, water chestnuts, mushrooms, sprouts and celery; cook till crisp-tender. Return onions to wok. Stir beer-cornstarch mixture; add all at once to meat-vegetable mixture. Cook and stir till bubbly; cook 2 minutes more. Turn out onto noodles. Sprinkle with walnuts and parsley. Serves 6 to 8.

## SAVORY QUAIL

- 8 4- to 6-ounce ready-
  to-cook quail
- ¼ cup all-purpose flour
- 2 tablespoons butter
- 1 12-ounce can *Coors*
  beer
- 2 tablespoons sliced
  green onion

Tie legs of each quail together with string; twist wings under back. In plastic bag combine flour, 1 teaspoon *salt* and ⅛ teaspoon *pepper*. Add quail 2 or 3 at a time; shake well to coat. Brown quail slowly in butter. Add Coors and onion. Cover and simmer till tender, 25 to 30 minutes. Remove quail to platter; remove strings and keep warm. Skim fat from drippings. Over high heat, reduce drippings to ¾ cup, about 3 minutes. Spoon sauce over birds. Serves 4.

*Meat & Wild Game*

# WESTERN SALOONS

Saloons offered thirsty Westerners drink, rest and conversation. Tents often served as drinking establishments in the mining towns which seemed to spring up overnight during the Gold Rush. If the town remained populated, tents would be replaced by permanent structures. Wood-frame saloons blossomed into opulent emporiums.

After months in the wilderness, many a cowboy, miner, lumberjack or trapper would visit town for both supplies and recreation. Drinking, whooping it up with the dance-hall ladies and playing poker could quickly empty the pockets of these fun-seeking settlers. Beer and whiskey inspired this drinking saying:

> One drink of it tempts you to
> steal your own clothes;
> Two drinks makes you bite off your
> own ears;
> And three will make you save your
> drowning mother-in-law.

Many of the early drinking establishments became legendary. One of the most famous saloon legends — the face on the barroom floor — evolved in the bar of the century-old Teller House Hotel in Central City, Colorado. According to the legend, a half-frozen miner stumbled in one night and tearfully painted his sweetheart's likeness on the floor. In fact, the painting was done in the early 1900s by Denver artist Herndon Davis, in the likeness of his wife. The painting still exists today.

## CHILI PIE WITH CORNMEAL DUMPLINGS

1½  pounds beef stew meat, cut into ¾-inch cubes
1  cup chopped onion
1  15½-ounce can red kidney beans, drained
1  12-ounce can *Coors* beer
1  8-ounce can tomatoes, cut up
¼  cup tomato paste
1  4-ounce can chopped green chilies
2  cloves garlic, minced
1  tablespoon chili powder
½  teaspoon ground cumin
¾  cup yellow cornmeal
¼  cup all-purpose flour
½  teaspoon baking powder
2  tablespoons cooking oil
1  beaten egg
⅓  cup milk

Place meat, onion and kidney beans in bottom of ungreased 3-quart casserole. In bowl combine Coors, undrained tomatoes, tomato paste, the undrained chilies, the garlic, chili powder, 1 teaspoon *salt* and the ground cumin. Pour over meat. Bake, covered, in 350° oven for 2 hours. Combine cornmeal, flour, baking powder and ¼ teaspoon *salt*. Stir in oil, egg and milk. Drop by tablespoonfuls onto hot stew, forming 8 dumplings. Bake, covered, 30 minutes more or till dumplings are done. Makes 8 servings.

*Some pioneers referred to deer or antelope as buckskin. This dish was a real treat for breakfast served with hot biscuits and chokecherry jelly.*

## BUCKSKIN AND GRAVY

- 1 **pound venison or antelope steak, cut ½ inch thick**
- 4 **slices bacon**
- ½ **cup chopped onion**
- ½ **cup all-purpose flour**
- 1 **cup milk**
- 1 **cup _Coors_ beer**

Pound venison to ¼-inch thickness. Cook bacon till crisp; drain, reserving drippings. Cook onion in drippings till tender; set aside. Combine flour, ½ teaspoon *salt* and ¼ teaspoon *pepper*; coat meat with flour mixture. Slowly brown meat on both sides in drippings till done, about 10 minutes. Remove meat; blend remaining flour from meat coating into drippings. Stir in milk, then Coors. Cook and stir till thickened; cook 1 to 2 minutes more. Season to taste. To serve, spoon gravy over meat and sprinkle with bacon. Serves 4.

## PHEASANT WITH APPLES
*(pictured right)*

- ¼ **cup all-purpose flour**
- 2 **2- to 3-pound ready-to-cook pheasants, cut up**

---

- ¼ **cup butter**
- ¾ **cup _Coors_ beer**
- ¾ **cup light cream**
- 3 **egg yolks**
  **Snipped parsley**

Combine flour, ½ teaspoon *salt* and ¼ teaspoon *pepper*. Coat pheasant with mixture; brown lightly in butter. Add Coors; simmer, covered, till tender, 45 to 55 minutes. Remove to platter. Beat cream with egg yolks. Stir into pan drippings; cook and stir over medium-low heat just till thickened. Do not boil. Serve with sauce; garnish with parsley. Serve with *Sautéed Apples:* Combine 2 *apples*, cored and cut into wedges, and 2 tablespoons *butter*. Sprinkle with 1 teaspoon *brown sugar*. Cook till lightly browned, 4 to 5 minutes. Serves 8.

 *"Belly Cheater" was one of many names for the cook.*

## BELLY CHEATER'S BRISKET

- 1 **3- to 4-pound fresh beef brisket**
- 3 **medium onions, sliced**
- 1 **12-ounce can _Coors_ beer**
- 1 **tablespoon brown sugar**
- 2 **teaspoons instant beef bouillon granules**
- 4 **whole black peppercorns**
- 1 **clove garlic, minced**
- 1 **bay leaf**
- ¼ **teaspoon dried thyme, crushed**
- ¼ **cup all-purpose flour**

---

## MOUNTAIN MEN'S GRUB

An unusual and favorite dish of the mountain men in the West was known by a French name — *boudin.*

An early version of boudin combined tender meat (usually from the buffalo) and entrails with suet and flour. The mixture traditionally was cooked over an open fire, using an organ from the animal (such as the stomach) as the cooking vessel.

Trim fat from brisket. Season meat with a little *salt* and *pepper*. Place in baking pan; cover with onion. Reserve ⅓ cup Coors. Combine remaining Coors, the brown sugar, bouillon granules and spices; pour over meat. Cover with foil. Bake at 350° for 3 to 3½ hours or till meat is tender. Remove meat. Skim off fat from pan juices; remove bay leaf. In saucepan cook juices down to 2 cups. Combine reserved Coors and flour; stir into pan juices. Cook and stir till thickened. Cook 1 to 2 minutes more. Season to taste. Slice meat across the grain; pass gravy. Serves 10.

**Pheasant with Apples**

## SMOTHERED BEAR STEAK

2¼ cups *Coors* beer
1 large onion, sliced
6 tablespoons cooking oil
2 tablespoons Worces-
    tershire sauce
2 cloves garlic, minced
3 pounds bone-in
    bear steak
½ cup beef broth
1 8-ounce can
    tomatoes, cut up
½ cup chopped carrot
½ cup chopped celery
½ teaspoon dried basil,
    crushed
½ teaspoon prepared
    mustard
2 tablespoons corn-
    starch
    Hot cooked noodles

Combine *1½ cups* of the Coors, onion, *4 tablespoons* of the oil, Worcestershire and garlic. Pierce meat with fork; place in plastic bag in shallow pan. Pour marinade over; seal bag. Chill several hours, turning occasionally. Drain; discard marinade. Brown meat on both sides in the 2 tablespoons hot oil. Add ¾ cup Coors, beef broth, tomatoes, carrot, celery, basil, mustard, ½ teaspoon *salt* and ⅛ teaspoon *pepper*. Bring to boiling. Reduce heat and simmer, covered, for 1½ hours or till tender. Transfer meat to platter. Skim fat from pan juices. Blend cornstarch and 2 tablespoons *water;* stir into pan juices. Cook and stir till thickened; cook 1 to 2 minutes more. Serve with noodles. Serves 4.

# COME AGAIN?

Variations of English were common in the West. People found their own shortcuts and expressions to aid communication. Regions developed their own phrases and pronunciations influenced by the ethnic backgrounds of the people.

Journals and other writings from the era of the mountain men reveal a language now needing a code book to translate:

*Possibles* were the provisions, clothing, ammunition that a trapper could get in exchange for his pelts.

*Up to beaver* was a compliment. It meant "smart." And it was true that you had to be cagey to trap the beaver.

*Make meat* referred to laying in a store of provisions by hunting.

*Grease hungry* let everyone know you had a craving for meat.

An example of an entire mountain-talk sentence:

*"Well, hos! I'll dock off buffler, and then if thar's any meat that runs that can take the shine outen dog, you can slide."*

Roughly translated:

"Well, friend, I'll accept some of your buffalo meat . . . but if you think there's any game out here that's better than dog, you're out of your mind."

## GRILLED STEAK AND PEPPERS

- 1½ pounds beef sirloin steak, cut 1 inch thick
- 2 cups *Coors* beer
- 2 tablespoons butter or margarine
- 2 cloves garlic, minced
- 1 large onion, sliced and separated into rings
- 1 medium sweet red pepper, cut into strips
- 8 ounces fresh mushrooms, halved
- ¾ teaspoon dried basil, crushed
- ¼ teaspoon pepper
- 4 teaspoons cornstarch
- 2 teaspoons sugar
- ½ cup chicken broth
- 1 4-ounce can whole green chili peppers, drained, seeded and cut into ½-inch strips
- 6 ¾-inch-thick slices *Coors* Sourdough French Bread, toasted (see recipe, page 74)

Trim excess fat from steak; discard trimmings. Place steak in shallow dish. Pour *1 cup* of the Coors over steak. Cover, refrigerate several hours or overnight, turning occasionally.

In skillet melt butter; add garlic and cook for 30 seconds. Add onion, red pepper, mushrooms, basil and pepper. Cook and stir about 5 minutes or till tender. Combine cornstarch and sugar. Stir some of remaining Coors into cornstarch mixture; stir cornstarch mixture, Coors and broth into vegetables in skillet. Cook and stir till bubbly; cook and stir 1 minute more. Stir in chili peppers; heat through.

Sprinkle steak with *salt* and *pepper*. Grill over *medium* coals, turning once (allow 20 to 25 minutes total for medium-rare). Slice steak across the grain into 1-inch-thick slices. Place 1 slice of Sourdough French Bread on each plate. Place several slices of steak atop the bread; top with some of the hot beer-vegetable mixture. Makes 6 servings.

 *Marinate flank steak in beer, then grill and serve slices rolled in warm flour tortillas with guacamole, onions and Pico de Gallo Salsa. The name of this peppery sauce means "beak of the rooster" in Spanish.*

## FAJITAS

- 1½ pounds beef flank steak
- 1 12-ounce can *Coors* beer
- 2 tablespoons cooking oil
- 1 tablespoon coarsely ground black pepper
- 2 teaspoons lime juice
- 2 cloves garlic, minced
- ½ teaspoon dried oregano, crushed
- 24 6-inch flour tortillas
- 1 large onion, chopped
- 2 tablespoons butter or margarine
- 1 16-ounce can refried beans, warmed
- 2 cups Original Guacamole (see recipe, page 74)
- Pico de Gallo Salsa

Trim excess fat from steak; place meat in plastic bag in bowl. In measuring cup combine Coors, cooking oil, pepper, lime juice, garlic and oregano; pour over steak. Cover; refrigerate overnight, turning bag occasionally.

Drain steak, reserving marinade. Pat steak dry with paper toweling. On covered grill cook steak directly over *medium-hot* coals 8 to 10 minutes, brushing meat occasionally with marinade. Turn; grill to desired doneness, allowing 8 to 10 minutes more for medium. Carve meat across grain in thin slices.

Wrap tortillas in foil; warm in 350° oven 8 to 10 minutes. In skillet cook onion in butter till tender. Wrap steak slices in tortillas spread with refried beans. Top with guacamole, chopped onion and Pico de Gallo Salsa. Serves 8.

**Pico de Gallo Salsa:** In bowl combine 3 medium *tomatoes*, peeled and chopped; ½ cup sliced *green onions*; 1 chopped *fresh serrano or jalapeño chili pepper*; 1 tablespoon chopped *cilantro or parsley*; 1 teaspoon *lime juice* and ½ teaspoon *salt*. Chill. Makes 2 cups.

*Meat & Wild Game*

## TACOS AL CARBON

*(pictured on the cover)*

- 1 12-ounce can *Coors* beer
- 2 cloves garlic, minced
- 1½ teaspoons sugar
- 1½ teaspoons dried oregano, crushed
- 1 bay leaf
- 2 tablespoons lemon juice
- 1 tablespoon lime juice
- ½ teaspoon sesame oil
- 1¼ pounds beef flank steak
- 2 large avocados, halved, seeded and peeled
- 1 cup chopped tomatoes
- 2 tablespoons snipped cilantro or parsley
- 2 tablespoons chopped green onion
- 2 tablespoons lime juice
- 2 to 4 finely chopped fresh green serrano chili peppers
- ½ teaspoon salt
- ½ cup chopped tomatillos (optional)
- 1 tablespoon cooking oil
- 12 6-inch corn tortillas
  Salsa
  Dairy sour cream

For marinade, in shallow bowl combine Coors, garlic, sugar, oregano, bay leaf, lemon juice, the 1 tablespoon lime juice and sesame oil. Cut flank steak into 4-inch-long strips, 1 inch wide and ¼ inch thick. Add meat to the marinade. Cover and marinate meat strips in refrigerator for 6 hours, stirring the meat occasionally.

For guacamole, about 1 hour before serving, in mixing bowl mash avocados. Stir in tomatoes, cilantro, onion, 2 tablespoons lime juice, chili peppers, salt and tomatillos, if desired. Cover; let stand at room temperature for 1 hour before serving.

Remove meat strips from marinade. In large skillet cook meat strips, half at a time, in hot oil for 2 or 3 minutes or till meat is just done. Keep warm.

Meanwhile, wrap tortillas in foil. Place in 350° oven for 10 minutes or till heated through.

To serve, place a few meat strips on each tortilla; top with about 2 *tablespoons* guacamole. Roll the tortilla around meat and guacamole. Serve with remaining guacamole, salsa and sour cream dolloped atop. Makes 4 to 6 servings.

## MONTANA STEAK AND ONIONS

*(pictured right)*

- 1 beef sirloin steak, cut 1½ inches thick (2 to 2½ pounds)
- ¼ cup *Coors* beer
- 2 tablespoons Worcestershire sauce
- 1 large onion, sliced and separated into rings
- 1 sweet red or green pepper, cut into strips
- 2 cups sliced fresh mushrooms
- 1 large clove garlic, minced
- ¼ teaspoon celery salt
- ¼ cup butter

Slash fat edges of steak at 1-inch intervals (don't cut into meat). Combine Coors and Worcestershire; brush onto meat. Grill over medium-hot coals for 8 to 10 minutes, brushing often with Coors mixture. Turn; grill 8 to 10 minutes more for rare doneness, brushing often with Coors mixture. Or, broil steak 3 inches from heat for 14 to 16 minutes, turning once. In skillet cook onion, sweet pepper, mushrooms, garlic and celery salt in butter till vegetables are tender. Spoon vegetables atop meat. Slice steak across grain to serve. Serves 6.

# PRAIRIE SCHOONERS

The Conestoga wagon was the primary means of transportation for pioneers going West. It featured a massive boat-shaped body, with a hooped canvas covering. The wagon box was even watertight so it could float across a river. Little wonder this vehicle became known as the prairie schooner.

Six yoked pairs of oxen were needed to move a fully loaded Conestoga, which could carry three to four tons of supplies and possessions.

Montana Steak and Onions

Rivers

Rivers. They took lives and inspired songs, watered fields and flooded farms. Their fish and wild game gave life to hungry gold panners and trailblazers, and their banks, rich with minerals, fed valleys of crops. They spilled into the Pacific Ocean and the Gulf of Mexico where salt water yielded still more food for the West. Above all, the rivers rolled on, a symbol of permanence and inspiration to those who created order in the western wilderness.

There's not a log to make a
    seat
Along the river Platte,
So when you eat, you've got to
    stand
Or sit down square and flat.
It's fun to cook with buffalo
    chips,
Take one that's newly born.
If I knew once what I know now,
I'd have gone around the Horn.
    — A Pioneer
    From Alistair Cooke's *America*

## Life Along the Rivers

For some of the earliest pioneers, rivers were an obstacle to overcome. Spanish *vaqueros* from California slogged their way across the Rio Grande to rope cattle on the plains. Settlers heading west forded the Columbia, Green, Colorado and others with wagons and belongings, discovering that western rivers were often swifter and more treacherous than eastern rivers.

Despite the hardships they brought, rivers became a source of life. They provided transportation, food, water for farming and drinking, and sometimes, wealth. Placer miners panned for gold along the mountain streams and riverbeds. The Chinese turned the tule swamps of the San Joaquin River into rich farmland. Steamboats plowed the mighty Missouri, taking settlers into strange new territories.

Along the way there were rapids and flash floods that could sink a raft or give rise to a ballad. Whatever else they were, the rivers were never dull.

Rivers were the center of commercial activity in the early West. Boatmen maneuvered small craft such as *pirogues*, *bateaus*, canoes and skiffs around snags and sandbars to deliver goods to tiny communities. Flatboats, arks, broadhorns, rafts and keelboats plied the rivers next, using tin horns on foggy days to warn other craft of their presence. Finally, the steamboat drove out the smaller boats, moving larger equipment and droves of pioneers to settle the territories along the riverbanks.

Those who chose life along the rivers adapted quickly. Indians taught them to fertilize corn by burying river fish beneath corn plants to enrich the soil. A Montana settler reported a harvest of 30-pound turnips and oats running 160 bushels to the acre, owing to the rich soil and good water of the region.

Western rivers and streams provided another raw material for growing industry — water for brewing beer. Breweries sprang up quickly in the second half of the 19th Century. In 1850, there were 431 breweries nationwide. By 1860, the number had jumped to 1,262. In addition, home brewing was common. Beer became so popular that western folk songs, such as *Wild, Ripplin' Water*, pictured cowboys swigging beer as they wound down from a long haul or sat by the banks of a roaring river.

Beer's abundance meant that it was often substituted for water, as fresh water was not always available. It was a forerunner of coffee as a breakfast drink in some areas, although coffee was soon a staple in western chuck wagons. Ales and beer were popular accompaniments to food, and some folks swore that as a tonic, beer couldn't be beat.

## River Food

For pioneers on the long journey west, the "wild, ripplin' water" of the western rivers offered the delicacy of fresh fish — a welcome relief to a bland diet.

Fish were panfried, broiled on sticks, cooked on planks over a campfire, or salted and preserved. Aspen wood, hickory or apple tree branches were used to build covered boxes for "smoke cooking." The fish was impaled on a green branch inside the box, and the box was placed over a fire to smoke.

# NATIVE AMERICANS

Western Indian tribes had learned to survive in the hostile territory centuries before the first white settlers came to the new land. They were clever and resourceful in stalking game, growing vegetables, preparing food and in communicating with each other.

One example of Indian ingenuity was a unique method of cooking in watertight woven baskets and colorfully painted pottery. The baskets were flammable and the pottery could not withstand the direct heat of a fire. The problem was solved by placing water and raw food in both types of vessels and then adding red-hot stones to boil the food.

One of the boiled dishes which came from this method of cooking was made of fish, corn and beans which they called succotash. Later, the fish was omitted, creating the vegetarian version of succotash known today.

Another example of the Indians' cleverness was their method of harvesting wild rice which grew along river marshes. A small boat was poled through marshes where heavy-headed rice stalks swayed over the boat. Indians beat the stalks with a club to free the rice grains, and stamped on them to loosen the hulls. To blow away the hulls they tossed the grains over blankets or birch trays, and stored the rice in a hole lined with animal skins.

Fishing was a necessity along the rivers. An old rule of thumb for a sure catch advised fishermen to "Take the juice of smallage (wild celery or parsley) or lovage (a European domestic herb) and mix with any kind of bait. As long as there remains any kind of fish within yards of your hook, you will find yourself busy pulling them out."

— From *In Grandmother's Day: A Legacy of Recipes, Remedies, and Country Wisdom from 100 Years Ago,* by Jean Cross.

Farmers along rivers often lived off only fish, poultry and eggs while they cleared their land for crops. This limited diet gave rise to a variety of recipes. Spanish settlers contributed chile and jalapeño peppers for *huevos rancheros* and other hot dishes. Northern farmers adapted the Scandinavian lye-cured cod dish called *lutefisk.* Pickled herring was another Scandinavian favorite, while the Mexican version of fish pickling incorporated lime juice with a hint of coriander for a dish named *ceviche*.

Wild birds such as the prairie hen, duck, wild turkey, goose and sharp-tailed grouse also thrived near water where they hid in the tall grass and nested in sloughs and ponds. Skillet braising of this ready source of food was common. Pheasant, often thought of as a frontier dish, was never seen in America until 1880 when it was brought to the new land from China.

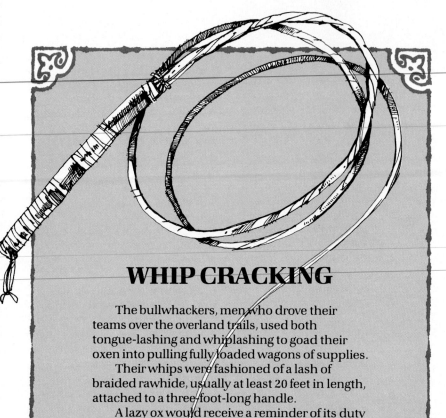

# WHIP CRACKING

The bullwhackers, men who drove their teams over the overland trails, used both tongue-lashing and whiplashing to goad their oxen into pulling fully loaded wagons of supplies.

Their whips were fashioned of a lash of braided rawhide, usually at least 20 feet in length, attached to a three-foot-long handle.

A lazy ox would receive a reminder of its duty in the form of a whack on its flank, accompanied by a volley of curses that would prod the rest of the team as well.

The whip could also work to the oxen's benefit. A bullwhacker who spotted a rattlesnake along the trail could kill it with a whiplash from eight paces before the snake could strike.

Bullwhackers flaunted their skill with a great deal of showmanship. Often, one man would attempt to take a friend's coin off the top of a stake in the ground with a flick of the whip. If he knocked the coin off cleanly he could keep the money.

 *During the 1880s, social service clubs such as the Elks built fancy meeting halls and dining rooms in small western towns. This was a popular dish served.*

## GOLDEN BUCKS

- ¾ cup *Coors* beer
- 1 tablespoon Worcestershire sauce
- ½ teaspoon dry mustard Dash ground red pepper
- 1½ cups shredded sharp cheddar cheese
- 1½ cups shredded American cheese
- 1 tablespoon all-purpose flour
- 6 eggs Butter or margarine
- 6 slices bread, toasted

In medium saucepan heat together beer, Worcestershire, mustard and red pepper. Toss together cheeses and flour. Over medium-low heat gradually stir cheeses into beer mixture, stirring constantly till cheeses are melted and mixture just begins to bubble; keep warm. In skillet fry eggs in butter to desired doneness. On each plate place 1 slice of toast. Top with some cheese sauce and 1 egg. Sprinkle with *paprika* and *parsley,* if desired. Serve immediately. Serves 6.

*Fish, Poultry & Eggs*

*Note:* You can substitute 6 ounces commercial noodles for the homemade noodles.

## BACON-WRAPPED TROUT
*(pictured right)*

  1  **15-ounce can tomato sauce**
  ½  **cup *Coors* beer**
  ¼  **cup butter or margarine**
  2  **tablespoons lemon juice**
  2  **tablespoons chopped green onion**
  1  **teaspoon sugar**
  1  **teaspoon dried salad herbs**
  ½  **teaspoon salt**
     **Few drops bottled hot pepper sauce**
  6  **whole pan-dressed trout (about 5 ounces each)**
 12  **slices bacon, cooked about 5 minutes**

In small saucepan combine tomato sauce, Coors, butter or margarine, lemon juice, green onion, sugar, salad herbs, salt and bottled hot pepper sauce. Simmer, uncovered, for 10 to 15 minutes; set aside. Thaw fish, if frozen. Wrap each fish in 2 slices bacon; secure with small skewers or wooden picks. Place on grill; cook 6 minutes on each side or till fish flakes easily when tested with a fork. Brush often with sauce during last few minutes of cooking. Pass warm sauce with fish. Serves 6.

**Bacon-Wrapped Trout**

Planked Salmon

 *Planks used for cooking should be made of unfinished hardwood — oak, maple and hickory are best. Before preparing the fish, season the plank by brushing it with cooking oil and heating in a 300° oven for 1 hour.*

## PLANKED SALMON

*(pictured left)*

- 1 **4- to 5-pound dressed salmon (without head)**
- 2 **tablespoons butter or margarine**
- 6 **medium potatoes, peeled and quartered**
- 2 **tablespoons butter**
- ¼ **teaspoon salt**
  **Dash pepper**
- 1 **slightly beaten egg**
- ¼ **cup milk, heated**
- 2 **tablespoons butter or margarine, melted**

Rinse fish and pat dry. Place in greased 15½x10½x2-inch baking pan. Brush first 2 tablespoons butter on inside and outside of fish; sprinkle fish cavity with a little *salt* and *pepper*. Bake in 400° oven about 50 minutes, or just till fish flakes with a fork. (Start checking after 35 minutes.) Meanwhile cook potatoes in boiling salted water for 25 to 30 minutes or till tender; drain. Mash potatoes; add the second 2 tablespoons butter, the salt and pepper. Cool slightly.

Beat in egg. Gradually add enough milk to make light and fluffy. Transfer salmon to 1½-inch-thick seasoned wooden plank larger than salmon. Using pastry tube and large star tip, pipe potatoes around salmon. Brush with 2 tablespoons melted butter. Bake 15 minutes more or till fish flakes easily when tested with a fork. Makes 8 to 10 servings.

## TACOS VERDE, BLANCO Y ROJO

- 1 **small onion, chopped**
- 3 **tablespoons cooking oil**
- 1 **8-ounce can tomato sauce**
- ½ **teaspoon crushed red pepper**
- ¼ **teaspoon salt**
- 2 **cups chopped cooked chicken**
- 12 **6-inch corn tortillas**
- 2 **cups mashed avocado**
- ½ **cup dairy sour cream**

Cook onion in *1 tablespoon* of the oil till tender; stir in tomato sauce, pepper and salt. Simmer, covered, for 5 minutes. Stir in chicken; heat through. Keep warm. In small skillet heat the remaining 2 tablespoons oil. Dip each tortilla in hot oil for 10 seconds or just till limp. Drain on paper toweling. Spoon a little avocado, sour cream and meat mixture onto one half of each tortilla. Fold other half over filling; serve immediately. Makes 6 servings.

*Fish, Poultry & Eggs*

## HUEVOS MOTULEÑOS

1¼ cups dry black
    beans (8 ounces)
2 cups *Coors* beer
¼ cup chopped onion
1 clove garlic, minced
1 8-ounce can
    tomatoes, finely
    chopped
2 tablespoons finely
    chopped onion
⅛ teaspoon cayenne
    Cooking oil
1 10-ounce package
    frozen peas
1½ cups diced fully
    cooked ham
8 6-inch corn tortillas
8 eggs
½ cup shredded
    Monterey Jack
    cheese (2 ounces)

Rinse beans. In large saucepan soak beans overnight in 3 cups *water*. (Or, bring to boiling; simmer 2 minutes. Cover and let stand 1 hour.) Drain. Add Coors, the ¼ cup onion, garlic and 1 teaspoon *salt*; cook, covered, for 2½ to 3 hours or till beans are very tender. Combine *undrained* tomatoes, the 2 tablespoons onion, ½ teaspoon *salt* and the cayenne. Set aside. Heat *2 tablespoons* cooking oil in large heavy skillet. Add beans and liquid. Mash beans in skillet. Cook, uncovered, over medium heat for 3 to 5 minutes or till very thick. Cook peas according to package directions; drain. Toss with ham; cover and keep warm. Heat ¼ inch oil in another skillet. Fry tortillas 20 to 40 seconds per side or till crisp and golden. Drain on paper toweling. Spread about ⅓ cup bean mixture on each tortilla; keep warm in 300° oven. In same oil fry eggs till set. Season with a little salt and pepper. Place one atop each bean-covered tortilla. Sprinkle each with about ⅓ cup of ham-pea mixture. Spoon some of the tomato sauce atop. Sprinkle with cheese. Makes 8 servings.

## CHICKEN CHOP SUEY

2 chicken breasts,
    skinned and boned
1 large clove garlic,
    minced
1 teaspoon grated
    fresh gingerroot
¼ cup cooking oil
2 medium onions,
    sliced
2 cups sliced fresh
    mushrooms
2 cups fresh bean
    sprouts
¾ cup bias-sliced celery
½ cup sliced water
    chestnuts
⅓ cup chopped green
    pepper
¼ cup chopped canned
    pimiento
1 cup *Coors* beer
¼ cup soy sauce
½ teaspoon instant
    chicken bouillon
    granules
2 tablespoons cold
    water
4 teaspoons
    cornstarch
    Hot cooked rice

Cut chicken breasts into 2x½-inch strips. In large heavy skillet or wok cook garlic and gingerroot in *2 tablespoons* of the hot oil for 30 seconds. Add remaining oil. Add chicken; cook about 2 minutes, stirring constantly. Add next seven ingredients. Cook and stir 2 minutes more. Add Coors, soy sauce and bouillon granules. Bring mixture to boiling; cover and simmer 2 to 3 minutes. Blend cold water into corn-starch; stir into vegetable mixture. Cook, stirring constantly, till mixture is thickened and bubbly. Cook and stir 1 to 2 minutes more. Serve over hot cooked rice. Makes 6 servings.

## ROCKY MOUNTAIN TROUT

4 10- to 12-ounce
    cleaned fresh or
    frozen trout
    (heads on)
1 teaspoon salt
1 teaspoon paprika
¼ teaspoon pepper
1 cup cornmeal
    Shortening for frying

Thaw fish, if frozen; rinse and pat dry. Combine salt, paprika and pepper; rub over fish and in body cavity. Dip fish in cornmeal to coat both sides. In large skillet heat ¼ inch shortening. Add fish in single layer. Fry 6 to 7 min-utes per side, or till fish flakes easily with a fork. Drain on paper toweling. Makes 4 servings.

*Fish, Poultry & Eggs*

# HANGTOWN FRY

During California's frantic gold rush of the early 1850s, food prices in mining towns rose to unbelievable levels—usually in direct proportion to the amount of gold available in the area. In one town, for example, pieces of watermelon sold from $4 to $6 each. But food prices were of no concern to the fortunate few who struck it rich. According to one story, a lucky miner who had just found a bonanza at Shirttail Bend wandered into the area's only restaurant located in the Carey House Hotel in Hangtown. The miner demanded the most expensive meal on the menu. Eggs were a dollar each and oysters were even higher. The clever chef combined the two and created Hangtown Fry.

## HANGTOWN FRY

- 12 medium-sized shucked oysters
- 3 tablespoons all-purpose flour
- ½ teaspoon salt
  Dash pepper
- 1 beaten egg
- 2 tablespoons butter or margarine
- 6 eggs
- ⅓ cup milk
- ¼ teaspoon salt

Pat oysters dry with paper toweling. Combine flour, the ½ teaspoon salt and the pepper. Dip oysters into the 1 beaten egg, then into the flour mixture. In 10-inch skillet melt the butter or margarine over medium heat. Cook oysters in butter till edges curl, about 2 minutes on each side. Beat the 6 eggs with the milk and the ¼ teaspoon salt. Pour into skillet with oysters. As egg mixture begins to set on bottom and sides, lift and fold over with wide spatula. Continue cooking and folding for 4 to 5 minutes or till eggs are cooked throughout. Remove from heat. Makes 3 or 4 servings.

# SODDIES

Pioneers came from both the eastern United States and the rest of the world, making the long, difficult trip to settle on promising western land. Many discovered that much of the land was nothing more than treeless, open prairie with no wood for fuel or for building cabins.

Bent on survival, they learned that sod was a good building material.

After turning the sod so they could plant their root crops, they used the root-bound earth chunks as bricks to build houses. These ingenious buildings became known as soddies.

 *Actress Lillie Langtry was worshiped from afar by Texas hanging judge Roy Bean. Legend has it he never went anywhere without her photograph.*

## LILLIE LANGTRY BRUNCH

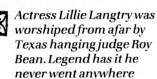

4 medium potatoes, peeled and diced
3 tablespoons butter
½ medium onion, chopped
1 jalapeño pepper, seeded and chopped
¼ cup salsa picante
1 teaspoon seasoned salt
1 teaspoon paprika
⅛ teaspoon pepper
4 eggs
1 cup *each* shredded sharp cheddar and Monterey Jack cheese

Cook potatoes in boiling water just till tender; drain. Melt butter in heavy skillet. Add onion and cook until tender. Add jalapeño and salsa. Stir and cook over low heat 2 minutes. Add potatoes, seasoned salt, paprika and pepper. Stir gently over low heat till potatoes are heated through. Poach, fry or scramble eggs (slightly undercook them, as they will continue cooking later). Season with salt and pepper. Divide potato mixture among 4 heatproof plates or ramekins. Top each with an egg. Combine cheeses; sprinkle over eggs. Place under broiler for 2 minutes or until cheese is melted. Serves 4.

## COLORADO OMELET

*(pictured right)*

1 medium tomato, peeled and cut up
1 4-ounce can green chilies, drained, seeded and rinsed
½ small onion, cut up
1 tablespoon snipped cilantro or parsley
1 tablespoon olive or cooking oil
2 dashes cayenne pepper
1 small clove garlic
1 small avocado, peeled and seeded
1 tablespoon mayonnaise
3 eggs
1 tablespoon water
2 tablespoons butter
1 8-inch flour tortilla
½ cup shredded Monterey Jack or cheddar cheese
Dairy sour cream

In blender container combine tomato, *half* the chilies, the onion, cilantro, oil, cayenne, garlic, ¼ teaspoon *salt* and a dash *pepper*. Cover and blend till nearly smooth. Pour into saucepan; bring to boiling. Reduce heat; cook and stir about 5 minutes or till slightly thickened. Keep warm. Mash avocado; stir in mayonnaise. Set aside. In bowl beat together eggs, water, ⅛ teaspoon *salt* and a dash *pepper*. Chop remaining chilies; stir into eggs. In 8-inch skillet with flared sides, heat butter. Lift and tilt pan to coat sides. Add egg mixture; cook over medium heat. As eggs set, run a spatula around skillet, lifting eggs to allow uncooked portion to flow underneath. When eggs are set, remove from heat. Place tortilla on plate; spread with avocado mixture. Sprinkle with ¼ *cup* of the cheese. Invert omelet atop. Roll up tortilla with omelet inside. Top with remaining cheese and a dollop of sour cream. Garnish with cilantro or parsley. Serve with tomato sauce. Makes 2 servings.

*Fish, Poultry & Eggs*

**Colorado Omelet**

*If self-rising flour and cornmeal are unavailable, add 1 teaspoon baking powder, ½ teaspoon salt and ½ teaspoon soda to each cup of all-purpose flour or cornmeal you use.*

## COUNTRY FRIED CATFISH

6   8-ounce fresh or frozen pan-dressed catfish or other fish
1   cup buttermilk
1   beaten egg
½   cup self-rising flour
¼   teaspoon salt
⅛   teaspoon pepper
1½   cups self-rising cornmeal
    Shortening or cooking oil for deep-fat frying

Thaw fish, if frozen; dry with paper toweling. In shallow bowl place ½ *cup* of the buttermilk. In another bowl combine egg with remaining ½ cup buttermilk. In another bowl stir together flour, salt and pepper. Dip fish first into buttermilk, then into flour mixture, then into egg mixture, and finally into the cornmeal to coat. In large saucepan or deep-fat fryer heat about 2 inches shortening to 365°. Fry fish 2 or 3 at a time for 5 to 7 minutes or till golden brown and fish flakes easily when tested with a fork. Drain fish on paper toweling; keep warm in 325° oven while frying the remaining fish. Makes 6 servings.

# BRONC BUSTERS

Bronc busting was a form of entertainment and competition, as well as a necessity, in the West.

Bronc riders could tame a wild horse for use on cattle drives or on a ranch, but they also had fun with their skill, often at a tenderfoot's expense.

An inexperienced bronc buster received more ridicule than sympathy. He learned bronc busting the hard way, given little advice beyond, "Stay with her."

In a flash the bronc could rid itself of a burdensome rider and the bruised and battered greenhorn would hear hoots and guffaws that he "hurt the ground" or was "rough on the bunch grass" when he landed.

The challenge could also have serious consequences. The bronc might be the one to do the busting as this old epitaph reveals:

William Jake Hall
Got a buck and a fall;
Killed dead as a slug,
By a Texas plug:
Born in Georgy,
'48 Anno Domini.

*Most Basques came to the West from the Pyrenees Mountains between Spain and France to work for American sheep ranchers as herders. Because these men often spent months in the mountains with their herd, the foods they prepared had to be simple and hearty.*

## BASQUE SHEPHERD'S PIE

- 4 **slices bacon**
- 2 **medium potatoes, peeled and thinly sliced**
- 2 **tablespoons sliced green onion**
- 1 **tablespoon finely snipped parsley**
- ⅛ **teaspoon dried thyme, crushed**
- 4 **eggs**
- 2 **tablespoons milk**

Cook bacon till crisp; drain, reserving 2 tablespoons drippings. Crumble bacon; set aside. In reserved drippings cook potatoes, onion, parsley, thyme, ¼ teaspoon *salt* and a dash *pepper*, covered, over low heat till potatoes are barely tender, 20 minutes, stirring carefully once or twice. Beat together eggs and milk; pour over potato mixture. Cook, covered, over very low heat till egg is set, 8 to 10 minutes. With a wide spatula loosen potatoes and slide out onto plate. Sprinkle crumbled bacon atop. Makes 2 servings.

## BEER BATTER SHRIMP

- 2 **cups all-purpose flour**
- 2 **teaspoons baking powder**
- 1 **teaspoon dried basil, crushed**
- 1 **egg**
- 1 **12-ounce can *Coors* beer**
- 2 **pounds fresh shrimp, shelled and deveined**
  **Cooking oil for deep-fat frying**

In mixing bowl combine flour, baking powder, basil, ½ teaspoon *salt* and ⅛ teaspoon *pepper*. In mixer bowl beat egg; blend in Coors. Sprinkle flour mixture over liquid; beat just till flour is moistened and large lumps disappear. *Do not stir batter after it is mixed.* Wash shrimp; pat dry. Dip into batter. Fry, a few at a time, in deep hot oil (375°) 3 to 4 minutes. Drain. Serves 6.

**For Beer Batter Chicken:** Simmer one 3- to 3½-pound broiler-fryer chicken, cut up, in salted water 20 minutes; drain. Dip into batter. Fry, a few at a time, in deep hot oil (350°) 5 minutes, turning once. (Regulate temperature so chicken fries at 325°.) Drain. Serves 6.

**For Beer Batter Vegetables:** Cut desired fresh vegetables into strips or pieces. Parboil vegetables in salted water 2 to 3 minutes. Drain. Dip into batter. Fry, a few at a time, in deep hot oil (375°) 3 to 4 minutes. Drain.

## DRUNKEN FISH

- 1 **3-pound dressed fresh or frozen red snapper (head removed)**
- ½ **cup chopped onion**
- 1 **clove garlic, minced**
- 2 **tablespoons olive oil**
- ⅔ **cup *Coors* beer**
- 3 **medium tomatoes, peeled, seeded and chopped**
- ¼ **cup snipped parsley**
- 1 **teaspoon sugar**
- ½ **teaspoon dried oregano, crushed**
- ½ **teaspoon crushed red pepper**
- ¼ **teaspoon ground cumin**
- ½ **cup sliced pimiento-stuffed olives**
- 1 **tablespoon cornstarch**

Thaw fish, if frozen. Cook onion and garlic in hot oil till tender. Add Coors, tomatoes, parsley, sugar, oregano, red pepper, cumin and ½ teaspoon *salt*. Bring to boiling; reduce heat. Cover and simmer 5 minutes. Place fish in greased 13x9x2-inch baking dish. Season cavity of fish with a little *salt* and *pepper*. Stir olives into tomato sauce; pour over fish. Cover; bake in 350° oven for 45 to 60 minutes. Remove fish to platter; keep warm. Combine cornstarch and 2 tablespoons *cold water*. In saucepan combine pan juices and cornstarch mixture. Cook and stir till bubbly; cook 1 minute more. Pass with fish. Makes 6 servings.

## CORN BREAD-STUFFED TROUT

- 1 3-pound fresh or frozen whole pan-dressed trout
- 1 cup crumbled dry corn bread
- 1 cup soft bread crumbs (1½ slices)
- ½ cup chopped celery
- ¼ cup finely chopped onion
- 2 tablespoons finely chopped green pepper
- ¼ teaspoon ground sage
- 3 tablespoons butter or margarine, melted

Thaw fish if frozen. Sprinkle generously with salt. Place in well-greased shallow baking pan. Combine corn bread, bread crumbs, celery, onion, green pepper, ½ teaspoon *salt*, the sage and dash *pepper*. Add ¼ cup *water* to bread mixture, tossing to coat. Stuff fish loosely with stuffing mixture. Brush generously with melted butter; cover with foil. Bake in 350° oven for 45 to 60 minutes. Makes 6 servings.

## SMOKED SALMON

- Hickory chips
- 1 8-pound whole dressed salmon (without head)
- ½ cup butter, melted

Soak hickory chips in enough water to cover about 1 hour

# SMOKING

Smoking was a popular way to preserve meat in the early West.

Meat, fish and poultry were often cured on racks set up over smoldering hickory fires.

Dutch and German settlers brought three-level smokehouses to the West. Big hams, turkey breasts and larger chunks of meat were suspended at the lowest level, close to the fire for heavy smoking. Bacon slabs were hung in the middle and sausages were lightly smoked at the top.

before grilling. Drain chips. In covered grill arrange slow coals around edge. Sprinkle dampened chips over coals. Place fish in foil pan on grill. Close hood. Grill till fish flakes easily with a fork, 1¼ to 1½ hours. Brush fish occasionally with melted butter. Sprinkle hickory chips over coals every 20 minutes. Serve with Coors Fish Sauce (below). Makes 16 servings.

## COORS FISH SAUCE

- 1 cup mayonnaise
- ¼ cup catsup
- ¼ cup *Coors* beer
- 1 tablespoon prepared mustard
- 1 tablespoon lemon juice
- 1 teaspoon prepared horseradish

Combine all ingredients. Chill. Serve with fish. Makes 1½ cups sauce.

## ARROZ CON POLLO
*(pictured right)*

- 1 2½- to 3-pound broiler-fryer chicken, cut up
- 2 tablespoons cooking oil

• • •

- 1½ cups long-grain rice
- 1 cup chopped onion
- 2 cloves garlic, minced
- 2 12-ounce cans *Coors* beer
- 1 8-ounce can tomatoes, cut up
- 1 tablespoon instant chicken bouillon granules
- ¼ teaspoon thread saffron, crushed
- 1 cup frozen peas
- 1 2-ounce can whole pimientos, drained cut into strips

Sprinkle chicken with a little *salt* and *pepper*; brown in hot oil. Remove chicken. Reserve 2 tablespoons drippings in pan. Add rice, onion and garlic; cook and stir till rice is golden. Add Coors, undrained tomatoes, bouillon granules, saffron, ½ teaspoon *salt* and ¼ teaspoon *pepper*. Bring to boiling; stir well. Place chicken atop rice. Cover; simmer 30 to 35 minutes. Add peas; cover; cook 5 minutes more. Garnish with pimiento. Makes 4 to 6 servings.

Arroz con Pollo

*Molé is a Mexican sauce made with chilies, onion and other ingredients, and served over poultry. This most famous molé contains bitter chocolate and spices.*

## CHICKEN IN MOLÉ SAUCE

- 1 2½-pound chicken, cut up
- 1 12-ounce can *Coors* beer
- ½ cup *Coors* beer
- 1 medium tomato, peeled, seeded and cut up
- ¼ cup chopped onion
- 1 4-ounce can green chilies, seeded, rinsed and cut up
- ¼ cup blanched almonds
- ¼ cup raisins
- 1 6-inch tortilla, cut up
- 1 tablespoon sesame seed
- 1 clove garlic, minced
- ¼ teaspoon crushed red pepper
- ¼ teaspoon ground coriander seed
- ⅛ teaspoon *each* crushed aniseed, ground cloves and ground cinnamon
- ¼ of 1-ounce square unsweetened chocolate, melted
- 2 tablespoons cooking oil

In Dutch oven combine chicken, the 1 can Coors and 1 teaspoon *salt*; add water to cover. Bring to boiling; simmer, covered, for 25 minutes or till just tender. Drain, reserving ¼ cup broth. Set aside. For Molé Sauce, in blender container combine reserved ¼ cup broth, the ½ cup Coors, tomato, onion, chilies, almonds, raisins, tortilla, sesame seed, garlic, red pepper, coriander, aniseed, cloves, cinnamon, ⅛ teaspoon *salt* and dash *pepper*. Cover and blend till nearly smooth. Stir in chocolate. In skillet brown cooked chicken pieces in hot oil; return to Dutch oven. Pour Molé Sauce over all. Cover; bake in 350° oven for 25 minutes. Makes 4 servings.

## BEER-BROILED SHRIMP

*(pictured right)*

- ¾ cup *Coors* beer
- 3 tablespoons cooking oil
- 2 tablespoons snipped parsley
- 4 teaspoons Worcestershire sauce
- 1 clove garlic, minced
- 2 pounds large shrimp, unshelled

Combine Coors, oil, parsley, Worcestershire, garlic, ½ teaspoon *salt* and ⅛ teaspoon *pepper*. Add shrimp; stir. Cover; let stand at room temperature for 1 hour. Drain, reserving marinade. Place shrimp on well-greased broiler rack; broil 4 to 5 inches from heat for 4 minutes. Turn; brush with marinade. Broil 2 to 4 minutes more or till bright pink. Makes 6 servings.

## PICKLED EGGS

- 1 12-ounce can *Coors* beer
- ⅔ cup vinegar
- 2 tablespoons sugar
- ½ teaspoon celery seed
- 1 clove garlic, halved
- 2 bay leaves
- 12 hard-cooked eggs, shells removed
- 1 small onion, sliced

In saucepan combine Coors, vinegar, sugar, celery seed, garlic, bay leaves and 1 teaspoon *salt*; simmer, covered, for 5 minutes. Cool to room temperature. In large deep container, combine eggs and onion; pour beer mixture over eggs. Cover; chill 3 to 4 days. Makes 12.

# LINGO

Early Westerners enriched their language by borrowing Spanish words.

*Buckaroo* comes from the word *vaquero* meaning cowboy.

*Chaps* was derived from *chaparreras,* a word for leather leg protectors.

*Hackamore* is *jáquima* in Spanish and means a riding halter.

*Lariat* refers to *la reata* which simply translated is "the rope."

*Ten-gallon hat* is derived from the Spanish word for braid, *galón,* which described high-crowned, wide-brimmed headwear.

**Beer-Broiled Shrimp**

Prairies

hen cowboys first rode onto the prairies, they could travel for days without seeing another human being. Parched lips and tongue, a sand-filled scalp and a stiff back were the cowboy's way of life. They beat their shirts between rocks to kill bugs and ate breakfast in the saddle to loosen up after sleeping on the hard-ground. Through hundreds of miles of cattle drives, they created new trails for the homesteaders heading West.

These people who turned prairies into a nation were hard-living folks who had simple goals . . . to build a homestead, to feed a family, to tend a garden, to move a cattle herd. Simple goals that demanded all their resources and courage and that added another chapter to American tradition.

## The Cowboy Cook

"A roundup cook is a sort of human that was kicked in the head by a brindle cow or a cross-grained mule when very young . . . Nobody with good sense could be a roundup cook . . . Takes a special talent to wrangle Dutch ovens and feed fifteen or twenty men that eat like walruses all hours of the day or night, right through wind, dirt, snow, cold, rain and mud . . . They're temperamental as wimmin too. Also, they is very cranky."

— A writer pennamed F. A. G. (From *The Prescott Courier*)

Cowboy cooks went by names such as Grub Worm, Vinegar Jim, Cold Bread Joe and Sallie. Their home was the prairie dust and their family a team of cowboys. They arose before dawn and worked late into the night. They were mean and tough, and everybody depended on them.

Cowboys woke to the sound of grub calls such as, "Grab it now, or I'll spit in the skillet." Breakfast was sourdough biscuits and Arbuckles coffee. The chuck wagon was loaded with frijoles (beans), lard, rice, pepper, baking powder, flour, baking soda and dried fruits. "Lick" (molasses) and bacon were there in good times, along with an assortment of pills, quinine water and calomel for injuries and illness.

Cooks had to be resourceful and make do with what they had. Story has it that one cook crisscrossed the Texas cattle trails and collected wild oregano, chili peppers, wild garlic and *skunk eggs* (onions). He mixed them with fresh killed beef or buffalo for the best chili in Texas. To see to it that his spices never ran short, he saved seeds and planted spice gardens along the trail in mesquite patches. Next time around he would collect his spices, hang them to dry and have a restored supply.

The cook was hard on everybody, but hardest on his helper, the *swamper*. The swamper was usually a down-and-out vagrant whom the cook generally called Louse. He

fetched wood and *prairie pancakes* for fuel until he got fed up, then moved on to work in town saloons, emptying spittoons and cleaning tables.

## The Settlers

More than a million people trekked across the dry plains of Kansas, Oklahoma and Nebraska before the completion of the railroad in 1869. After that, the numbers soared. They built shacks from soil where they found no trees, and as the Indians said, turned the sod upside down.

As communities formed and farms were established, the settlers shared tradition and enjoyed the bounty of the rich farmland. Still, they were frugal, using all they produced. Soups and stews allowed them to eat hearty and stay thrifty, and adapted well to the open hearth and black kettle on the coals.

Polish settlers introduced *Bigos,* a hunter's stew which, in their homeland, was made of bear after a long day's hunt. In the new land, Bigos was made with beef or pork using sauerkraut and seasonings for flavor.

Hungarians brought their *goulash* which literally means herdsman's meat. It was made from available meat and vegetables and could be cooked in an iron kettle until all the liquid evaporated. It could then be dried in the sun and stored in a skin until reheated with water.

Squashes were easy to grow and store, and those with heavier skins, such as the Hub-

# "POMPIONS"

One of the oldest foods in American history, the pumpkin played an important role in feeding the settlers moving West.

America discovered pumpkins from the Indians who traded pumpkin seeds with early Spanish settlers. They combined pumpkin seeds, almonds, cumin seeds, popped corn, garlic and chili to season sauces.

Soups, stews, griddle cakes, fritters, breads, puddings and cakes were among the uses early pioneers found for the beloved "pompion." Records also show pumpkins were used in brewing when ingredients were scarce and regular beer could not be made.

Pumpkin stew was a favorite, made in a variety of ways. A mixture of corn, beans, green peppers, beef or chicken and fruit were stewed in pumpkin juice and served on the table in a cooked, hollowed-out pumpkin. Pumpkins were also cut into pieces, boiled, seasoned and served in a dish that resembled baked apples.

The abundance and versatility of pumpkins even prompted one pioneer to create the saying,

"We have pumpkins at morning,
    pumpkins at noon,
"If it were not for pumpkins, we should
    be undone."

bard, could be stored for long periods in winter. Pumpkins also were popular as a vegetable and as an ingredient in desserts. Housewives even used pumpkin as a natural sweetener in place of sugar. It was obtained by boiling the pumpkin and distilling its syrup which was then used in cakes, pies and sauces.

Home breweries put beer on the table at home and in the kitchen for use in early cheese and beer concoctions. Saloons of all sizes and styles dotted towns and trails, catering to the thirsts of dry-throated railroad graders, gunsmiths and peddlers. On the range, cowboys often slaked their thirst with canned tomatoes. But in town they preferred beer and spirits, and it may have been the tomatoes that created the popular western drink, "Red Eye." Red Eyes are still made from beer, tomato juice and Worcestershire sauce.

One of the most famous taverns of the time was the Hollenberg Station, a combination inn, post office and market center on Cottonwood Creek in Hanover, Kansas. Gerat Hollenberg, a German immigrant, along with his wife, hosted thousands of travelers between 1857 and 1874 — including teamsters, lawmen, soldiers, salesmen, preachers and desperadoes. The inn was a designated stagecoach stop on the route west to Fort Kearny. It was also a home station for Pony Express riders who blazed across prairies and through the desert for 2,000 miles.

# WORTH ITS SALT

At times the price per pound was four times the cost for beef, but salt was a necessity on the western frontier. It was used by Indians and early settlers alike to preserve and season meat, fish, corn and many other foods.

On the Oregon and Santa Fe trails, meat placed in oak barrels filled with salt brine would stay fresh the entire trip. The most common meat was salt pork, also known as "overland trout" by early pioneers. Many other foods also would stay fresh with an application of salt.

Even eggs were preserved with salt, sometimes over an entire winter. In the fall, pioneer women would fill a barrel with layers of eggs standing on end in a bed of salt (the salt completely covering the eggs). When a recipe called for a fresh egg, the women simply removed it from the barrel. Often, this supply of eggs would hold out until spring when the hens would start laying again.

 *A special smoky-flavored chili pepper called a chipotle seasons this delicious Mexican-style stew, or caldo, from the village of Tlalpa. Miss Leona Wood, Kit Carson's granddaughter, remembered it from her childhood.*

## THE BOWL OF THE WIFE OF KIT CARSON

- 4 cups chicken broth
- 1 15-ounce can garbanzo beans, drained
- 1 cup cubed cooked chicken or turkey
- 1 cup cooked rice
- 1 or 2 whole chipotle chili peppers
- ½ teaspoon paprika
- ½ teaspoon dried oregano, crushed
- 1 cup cubed or shredded Monterey Jack cheese
- 1 medium avocado, peeled, seeded and sliced

In large saucepan bring broth to boiling. Stir in beans, chicken, rice, chili pepper, paprika and oregano. Cover and simmer 5 to 10 minutes. Remove chili pepper and discard. Ladle into soup bowls; top with cheese and slices of avocado. Makes 5 or 6 servings.

*"Bowl of red" is another name for a mighty hot chili.*

## GILA RIVER BOWL OF RED

(pictured right)

|        |                                              |
|-------:|----------------------------------------------|
| 5      | **slices bacon**                             |
| 8      | **ounces hot bulk pork sausage**             |
| 1½     | **pounds ground beef**                       |
| 1      | **cup chopped onion**                        |
| ½      | **cup chopped green pepper**                 |
| 1      | **clove garlic, crushed**                    |
| 1 or 2 | **dried red chili peppers, seeded and crumbled** |
| 2      | **jalapeño peppers, seeded and diced**       |
| 1 to 1½| **teaspoons chili powder**                   |
| ¼      | **teaspoon dried oregano**                   |
| 2      | **12-ounce cans *Coors* beer**               |
| 1      | **12-ounce can tomato paste**                |
| 1      | **16-ounce can pinto beans, drained**        |

Cook bacon till crisp; drain, crumble and set aside. Brown sausage. Drain, reserving 2 tablespoons drippings; set sausage aside. In reserved drippings brown ground beef, onion, green pepper and garlic. Add bacon, sausage, peppers, chili powder, oregano and ½ teaspoon *salt*. Stir in Coors and tomato paste. Bring to boiling; simmer, covered, 1½ hours. Add beans; simmer, covered, 30 minutes more. Serve with shredded cheese and chopped onion. Serves 6 to 8.

**Gila River Bowl of Red**

Short Ribs and Cornmeal Dumplings

## SHORT RIBS AND CORNMEAL DUMPLINGS

*(pictured left)*

      3  **pounds beef short ribs, cut into serving-size pieces**
      1  **medium onion, cut into thin wedges**
      1  **clove garlic, minced**
      1  **28-ounce can tomatoes, cut up**
      1  **12-ounce can *Coors* beer**
    ½  **teaspoon crushed red pepper**
      2  **tablespoons soy sauce**
      1  **tablespoon sugar**
    ¼  **teaspoon ground nutmeg**
    ½  **cup yellow cornmeal**
      1  **beaten egg**
    ½  **cup all-purpose flour**
      1  **teaspoon baking powder**
      1  **8-ounce can whole kernel corn, drained**

Trim excess fat from ribs. In Dutch oven brown ribs; season with *salt* and *pepper*. Remove ribs; drain fat, reserving 2 tablespoons. Add onion and garlic to reserved drippings; cook till onion is tender. Add next 6 ingredients, ¾ teaspoon *salt* and ¼ teaspoon *pepper*. Return meat to Dutch oven; bring to boiling. Reduce heat; simmer, covered, 1½ to 2 hours. Cool; skim off fat. Return to boiling. Meanwhile, for dumplings: combine cornmeal, ½ teaspoon *salt* and 1 cup *water*; bring to boiling. Cook and stir till thickened.

Remove from heat. Stir some cornmeal mixture into egg; return all to hot mixture. Stir together flour, baking powder and dash *pepper*. Add to cornmeal mixture; beat well. Stir in corn. Drop by rounded tablespoonfuls into boiling stew. Cover; simmer till dumplings are done, 10 to 12 minutes. Makes 8 servings.

## MEXICAN CHEESE SOUP

      2  **cups chicken broth**
      1  **cup *Coors* beer**
      1  **teaspoon dried oregano, crushed**
      1  **cup shredded cheddar cheese (4 ounces)**
      1  **cup shredded Monterey Jack cheese (4 ounces)**
      2  **tablespoons all-purpose flour**
      3  **egg yolks**
      1  **cup diced, cooked and peeled potatoes**
      1  **4-ounce can diced green chili peppers**
      1  **teaspoon dry mustard**
    ⅛  **teaspoon garlic powder**

Heat broth, Coors and oregano till mixture boils. Toss together cheeses and flour. Over low heat slowly add cheeses to broth, stirring till smooth. Stir *1 cup* of hot mixture into yolks; return all to pan. Cook and stir till mixture boils. Stir in remaining ingredients. Serves 4.

## FALL ROUNDUP STEW

- 1 to 1½ pounds beef short ribs, cut into serving-size pieces
- 2 12-ounce cans *Coors* beer
- ½ cup diced lean salt pork
- 1½ teaspoons salt
- ⅛ teaspoon pepper
- 1 2½- to 3-pound chicken, cut up
- 3 carrots, quartered
- 3 tomatoes, quartered
- 3 onions, quartered
- 3 potatoes, peeled and quartered
- ½ small head cabbage, cut into wedges
- ½ small winter squash or pumpkin, peeled and cut into 1-inch cubes (1 cup)
- 1 medium green pepper, chopped
- 3 tablespoons snipped parsley
- 1 clove garlic, minced

In 5-quart Dutch oven combine ribs, Coors, salt pork, salt, pepper and 2 cups *water*. Bring to boiling. Reduce heat; cover and simmer 1 hour. Add chicken; cover and simmer 25 minutes more. Add remaining ingredients; cover and simmer 30 to 35 minutes more or till vegetables are tender. Spoon off fat. Season to taste with additional salt and pepper. Remove meat and vegetables and arrange on platter. Serve broth in separate bowls. Makes 6 servings.

*The fish stew cioppino is said to have originated with the Italian or Portuguese fishermen in California. It is made with whatever fish or seafood is on hand.*

## CIOPPINO

- 1 pound fresh or frozen fish fillets
- 1 large green pepper, diced
- 2 tablespoons finely chopped onion
- 1 clove garlic, minced
- 1 tablespoon cooking oil
- 1 16-ounce can tomatoes, cut up
- 1 8-ounce can tomato sauce
- ½ cup *Coors* beer
- 3 tablespoons snipped parsley
- ¼ teaspoon dried oregano, crushed
- ¼ teaspoon dried basil, crushed
- 12 ounces frozen shrimp, peeled and deveined
- 1 6-ounce can minced clams

Thaw fish, if frozen. Remove any skin from fillets; cut fillets into 1-inch pieces; set aside. Cook green pepper, onion and garlic in hot oil till tender. Add undrained tomatoes, tomato sauce, Coors, parsley, oregano, basil, ½ teaspoon *salt* and dash *pepper*. Bring to boiling. Reduce heat; cover and simmer 20 minutes. Add fish, shrimp, and undrained clams. Bring to boil. Reduce heat; cover and simmer for 5 to 7 minutes. Makes 6 servings.

## VENISON CIDER STEW

- 2 pounds venison or beef stew meat, cut into 1-inch pieces
- 1 cup *Coors* beer
- ¼ cup all-purpose flour
- 2 teaspoons salt
- ¾ teaspoon dried thyme, crushed
- ¼ teaspoon pepper
- 3 tablespoons cooking oil
- 1 12-ounce can *Coors* beer
- 1 cup apple cider or apple juice
- 3 potatoes, peeled and cut into chunks
- 4 carrots, quartered
- 2 onions, sliced
- 1 stalk celery, cut into 1-inch slices

Marinate venison in the 1 cup Coors in the refrigerator for several hours, stirring occasionally. Drain; discard marinade. Combine flour, salt, thyme, and pepper; coat meat with mixture. Brown meat, half at a time, in hot oil. Drain off fat. Return all meat to pan. Stir in the can of Coors and the apple cider; cook and stir till mixture comes to boiling. Reduce heat; cover and simmer about 1¼ hours. Add vegetables. Cook 30 minutes more. Makes 6 servings.

# CHILI AND CHILIHEADS

General consensus has chili originating around 1850 with Texas trail cooks who were responsible for feeding hungry cowboys on long cattle drives. To make this spicy, rib-stickin' grub, the trail cook made good use of whatever meats were available — chicken, buffalo, rabbit and even rattlesnake. These meats were seasoned with fat and plenty of chili peppers and were boiled in a stew pot.

Today's chili lovers, or "chiliheads" as they're known in the West, take pride in their special recipes for the hot, spicy concoctions. An added spice or ingredient here and there can easily distinguish one cook's chili from another's. Many secrets abide, with some cooks vowing their recipes will die with them. Few of them agree on the "right" way to make chili, since there are as many chili recipes as there are longhorns in Texas.

One version of chili that is considered Texas-style uses chunks of meat instead of ground meat, with the beans served to the side instead of in the chili. It is a spicy meal that will satisfy any chilihead.

## COORS SPICY CHILI

- 2 strips bacon
- 2 pounds beef chuck, diced
- 2 12-ounce cans *Coors* beer
- 2 tablespoons chili powder
- 1 tablespoon dried oregano, crushed
- 1 tablespoon ground cumin
- ½ teaspoon cayenne pepper
- 2 teaspoons Worchestershire sauce
- 1 tablespoon cornmeal or masa harina
- Cooked pinto beans

In large saucepan cook bacon till crisp; drain, reserving drippings in pan. Crumble bacon; set aside. In drippings, brown meat. Add next 6 ingredients and 1 teaspoon *salt*. Bring to boiling; reduce heat. Simmer, covered, 45 minutes. Combine cornmeal and ¼ cup *water*. Stir into hot mixture; add crumbled bacon. Return to boiling. Reduce heat; simmer, covered, 15 minutes. Serve with beans. Makes 8 servings.

*Rabbit is available in the frozen food section of most large supermarkets. If unavailable, substitute chicken.*

## RABBIT STEW

1 **2-pound ready-to-cook rabbit, cut up**
2 **cups *Coors* beer**
2 **onions, sliced**
2 **slices bacon, cut up**
1½ **teaspoons dried rosemary, crushed**
½ **teaspoon dried basil, crushed**
2 **medium potatoes, peeled and cubed**
1 **16-ounce can tomatoes, cut up**
1 **8½-ounce can whole kernel corn, drained**
1 **8½-ounce can lima beans, drained**
2 **tablespoons all-purpose flour**

Place rabbit pieces in large kettle or Dutch oven. Add Coors, onions, bacon, rosemary, basil, 1½ teaspoons *salt* and ⅛ teaspoon *pepper*; bring to boiling. Reduce heat; cover and simmer for 45 minutes. Stir in potatoes, undrained tomatoes, corn and lima beans. Cover; simmer 30 minutes more or till meat is done and potatoes are tender. Blend together flour and ¼ cup *water*; stir into hot stew. Cook and stir till bubbly. Cook and stir 1 to 2 minutes more. Makes 6 servings.

## POZOLE

1½ **pounds pork, cut into ½-inch pieces**
2 **12-ounce cans *Coors* beer**
½ **cup chopped onion**
2 **16-ounce cans hominy, drained**
1 **10-ounce can tomatoes with green chilies**

Combine pork, Coors, 1 cup *water*, chopped onion and 1 teaspoon *salt*. Cover; simmer 1½ hours. Add hominy and undrained tomatoes. Cover;

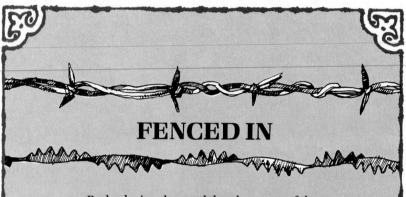

# FENCED IN

Barbed wire changed the character of the West, allowing landowners to establish well-defined boundaries for newly settled farms and ranches.

Elaborate wooden or stone fences or the thick shrubs with thorns used to form enclosures in the East simply would not work in the vast, open lands of the West.

Man-made thorns were invented in the early 1870s, and the use of this effective fencing grew like wildfire. While 5 tons of the prickly wire was produced in 1874, annual production in 1900 was 200,000 tons. The King Ranch alone had 1,500 miles of barbed wire fencing.

The rapid growth in the use of the wire created some problems. Cattle drives met blocked trails when settlers fenced off their precious water supply from others. Some towns were even cut off from other towns by cattlemen fencing in their ranges.

But the fencing protected new cropland, and it kept cattle from wandering and dying on the vast rangeland.

While barbed wire ended an era of open ranges, it helped develop the American agricultural system.

simmer 30 minutes more. Serve in bowls; top with shredded cabbage, sliced green onion, sliced radish, dried oregano, and crushed taco shells. Makes 6 to 8 servings.

## NAVAJO LAMB STEW

- 1 16-ounce can navy beans, drained
- 1 16-ounce can garbanzo beans, drained
- 1 pound boneless lamb, cut into ¾-inch cubes
- 1 12-ounce can *Coors* beer
- 1 cup chicken broth
- ½ cup chopped onion
- 1 clove garlic, minced
- ½ teaspoon salt
- ⅛ teaspoon pepper
- 3 medium potatoes or turnips, peeled and cubed (3 cups)
- 1 8-ounce can whole kernel corn, drained
- 2 tablespoons snipped parsley

In Dutch oven combine drained beans, lamb, Coors, broth, onion, garlic, salt and pepper. Bring to boiling. Cover and simmer 45 minutes or till lamb is nearly tender. Add potatoes or turnips and drained corn; simmer 15 minutes more or till vegetables and meat are done. Stir in parsley. Season to taste. Makes 8 servings.

## HAM AND BEAN VEGETABLE SOUP

- 1¼ cups dry navy beans (8 ounces)
- 6 cups water
- 2 12-ounce cans *Coors* beer
- 1½ cups water
- ¾ pound ham hocks
  • • •
- 1 medium potato, peeled and cubed (1 cup)
- 1 medium carrot, chopped (½ cup)
- 1 stalk celery, sliced (½ cup)
- 1 medium onion, chopped (½ cup)
- ½ teaspoon dried thyme, crushed
- ⅛ teaspoon pepper
  Few dashes bottled hot pepper sauce

Rinse beans. In 4½-quart Dutch oven combine beans and the 6 cups water. Bring to boiling; reduce heat and simmer 2 minutes. Remove from heat. Cover; let stand 1 hour. Drain.

Add Coors and the 1½ cups water; bring to boiling. Add ham hocks. Reduce heat; cover and simmer 1 hour or till beans are nearly tender. Remove ham hocks. Cut meat off bones and coarsely chop; discard bones. Return meat to soup along with the potato, carrot, celery, onion, thyme, pepper, and hot pepper sauce. Cover and simmer 30 minutes or till vegetables are tender. Season to taste with salt and pepper. Makes 6 servings.

## BEER BEEF STEW

- 1 pound beef stew meat, cut into 1-inch cubes
- 2 tablespoons cooking oil
- 1 12-ounce can *Coors* beer
- 1 teaspoon salt
- ⅛ teaspoon pepper
  • • •
- 1 7½-ounce can tomatoes
- 1 small onion, cut up
- 1 tablespoon sesame seed
- ½ teaspoon crushed dried red pepper
- 1 clove garlic
  • • •
- 1 medium zucchini, cut up
- 1 medium potato, peeled and cut up
- 2 ears fresh corn, cut into 1-inch pieces
- 1 tablespoon snipped parsley

In large saucepan brown meat in hot oil. Add Coors, salt and pepper. Cover and simmer for 1¼ hours.

In blender container place undrained tomatoes, onion, sesame seed, crushed red pepper and garlic; cover and blend till nearly smooth. Add to beef mixture along with zucchini, potato and corn. Cover and simmer 30 minutes or till meat is tender and vegetables are done. Season to taste with salt and pepper. Stir in parsley. Makes 4 servings.

Soups & Stews

## HERBED CHICKEN-VEGETABLE STEW

- 1 12-ounce can *Coors* beer
- 1½ cups chicken broth
- 1 10-ounce package frozen lima beans
- 1 8¾-ounce can cream-style corn
- 1 8-ounce can tomatoes, cut up
- 1 medium potato, peeled and diced (1 cup)
- 1 medium onion, chopped (½ cup)
- 1½ teaspoons sugar
- ½ teaspoon dried rosemary, crushed
- ¼ teaspoon pepper
- 1 bay leaf
- 1½ cups cubed cooked chicken

In 3-quart saucepan combine all ingredients *except* chicken. Bring to boiling; reduce heat. Cover and simmer 40 minutes. Add chicken; heat through. Season to taste. Remove bay leaf; discard. Serves 5 or 6.

## PIONEER STEW

- 6 slices bacon
- 1 onion, sliced
- 1 clove garlic, minced
- 1 pound beef shank crosscuts
- ¾ pound ham hock
- 2 12-ounce cans *Coors* beer
- 2 15-ounce cans garbanzo beans
- 4 potatoes, cubed

- 1 4-ounce link cooked Polish sausage, thinly sliced

Cook bacon till crisp; drain, reserving 2 tablespoons drippings. Crumble bacon and set aside. Add onion and garlic to reserved drippings in pan. Cook till tender. Add beef shank, ham hock, Coors, 1 cup *water* and 1 teaspoon *salt*. Heat to boiling. Reduce heat; cover and simmer 1½ hours. Remove meat from beef shank and ham hock; dice, discarding bones. Return meat to soup with undrained beans and potatoes. Cover and simmer 20 minutes more. Add sausage and crumbled bacon. Heat through. Skim off fat. Makes 8 to 10 servings.

## MEXICAN CHICKEN SOUP
*(pictured right)*

- 1 4½- to 5-pound stewing chicken, cut up
- 3 12-ounce cans *Coors* beer
- 1 small onion, sliced
- 3 stalks celery, cut up
- 1 16-ounce can tomatoes, cut up
- 3 medium carrots, thinly sliced
- 1 medium onion, chopped
- 4 teaspoons instant chicken bouillon granules
- 1 small zucchini, thinly sliced
- 1 cup frozen peas

Combine chicken, Coors, sliced onion, celery, 2 cups *water*, 1 teaspoon *salt* and ⅛ teaspoon *pepper*. Simmer, covered, for 2 to 2½ hours. Remove chicken from broth. Strain broth, discarding vegetables; skim fat. Combine broth, undrained tomatoes, carrots, chopped onion and bouillon granules; simmer, covered, 30 minutes. Remove and discard chicken skin and bones. Cube meat; add to broth along with zucchini and peas. Cover and simmer 10 to 15 minutes more. Garnish with *avocado slices*, if desired. Makes 10 servings.

## GUTSY

Saturday nights in border towns sometimes brought severe hangovers. A sure cure for this affliction was menudo, a Mexican stew containing hominy, tripe, pigs' feet, beef knuckles and calves' feet.

An American version of menudo is made with heart, liver, brains, tongue, kidneys and tripe. Its magic ingredient is marrow-gut — the tube connecting the two stomachs of cud-chewing animals.

Both stews indicate the scarcity of meat in the old West where people consumed virtually everything edible.

Mexican Chicken Soup

Deserts

To the Spanish conquistadores and pioneer padres who gradually migrated from Mexico into the western deserts, the arid canyons and flatlands offered excitement, adventure and plenty of danger. On the surface the desert was a dry, barren land baked by a relentless sun and yellowed by the dust of howling windstorms. Survival was a treacherous game, played against the rasping hiss of rattlesnakes and the roar of flash floods.

To live in the desert was to flirt with death. Yet these earliest explorers survived, finding in the parched land a new kind of excitement. They set examples for a stream of Mexican settlers and land speculators from other nations who would fight to claim the desert.

The Mexican War of 1846 established U.S. ownership, and the gates of the great American deserts opened to even more waves of new settlers who migrated from Mexico and the East. The Hispanic/Indian culture which had taken root centuries before remained dominant, reflecting the wisdom of the earliest survivors who had discovered the desert's secret of life.

### Southwest Deserts
To survive the drought and heat of the Chihuahuan, Sonoran and Mojave deserts, Spanish and Mexican settlers quickly adopted the foods and farming techniques of the Indians. Their lifeblood was the water from mountain rivers which carved great canyons and bubbled into tributaries and smaller streams which they used for irrigation.

Small settlements sprang up along the banks of these rivers. The Salt River, in what is now Arizona, yielded a fertile ribbon of cotton, alfalfa, grain, vegetables, melons and citrus. One settlement here flourished and was given the name Phoenix.

At first the deserts were populated by adventurers, gamblers and land speculators. Topographical engineers, army officers with their troops and families, mining and railroad promoters, merchants and politicians in search of untapped constituencies trickled into the lawless towns. A man such as Wyatt Earp could rise from a life of gambling to a life of law overnight. Or a man might have his life snuffed out in a shoot-out in the street with an angry desperado.

Settlements spread when pioneers learned to build canals to irrigate land located miles from a water source. Mining speculators found a wealth of copper and silver ore in parts of New Mexico and Arizona, and many unsuccessful California gold miners tried their luck in the desert territory. Some folks came when they heard the air was dry and the winters were mild.

Traveling through the deserts was hard business that took planning and work every step of the way. A pioneer woman gave a description of her daily chore of making "salt rising bread":

"When we camped I made [dough] and set it on the warm ground and it would be up about midnight. I'd get up and put it to sponge and in the morning, the first thing I did was to mix the dough and put it in the oven and by the time we had breakfast it would be ready to bake; then we had nice coals and by the time I got things washed up . . . the bread would be done and we would go on our way rejoicing."

—From *The American West*
The Forum Series in American History

### The California Desert
The arid land of south-central California was not always the fertile farming area that we know today. It was a barren desert when the first settlers arrived. Chinese immigrants along with Italians and Greeks slowly turned river valleys into productive gardens and introduced new vegetables and methods of cooking and seasoning.

Women who married into these ethnic communities often had to learn new cooking styles, using traditional methods and foods that were part of their husbands' heritage.

These food traditions popularized the artichoke, a favorite Italian food that was considered too difficult to eat by others.

These early settlers also showed others how minimal cooking could enhance vegeta-

# DEATH VALLEY SCOTTY

Most folks who saw Walter "Death Valley Scotty" Scott throwing money out hotel windows thought that he had struck it rich mining gold in Death Valley. But those who knew Scotty knew there was no gold in Death Valley and that Scotty was a confidence man without equal.

Scotty learned to survive by his wits at an early age. At 10, he had landed a job as a horse wrangler. By the time he was 12, he was driving 20-mule-team borax wagons across the Mojave desert. In 1888, at the age of 13, he was hired as a cowboy in Buffalo Bill Cody's Wild West Show.

After being fired from the show in 1900, Scotty convinced a gold-hungry New Yorker to finance a Death Valley prospecting expedition. Scotty spent at least $8,000 of the gullible man's money on a good time, but he didn't turn up a speck of gold. He went back to New York where he found millionaire Albert Johnson. Scotty's talk of Death Valley gold convinced Johnson to accompany Scotty on another prospecting trip.

Scotty got along on Johnson's generosity and money for years. In addition to tossing money out hotel windows, he once chartered an entire train for a trip from Los Angeles to Chicago. He even convinced Johnson to build a castle in Death Valley. Today the castle is a popular tourist attraction.

When he died in 1954, Death Valley Scotty became a tall-tale legend. He never did find pay dirt in Death Valley, but he found it in the pockets of unsuspecting men.

bles' flavor and preserve their freshness. Traditionally, vegetables were overcooked by Americans, but Chinese, Italians and Greeks insisted on crispness.

Other foods came to light in California deserts. A visitor during the 1880s found the region "a land of salads," although widespread use of salads elsewhere was not common until many years later.

### Desert Gardens and Food

Beans were plentiful in desert diets and pioneers ate varieties such as lima, sieva, curry, kidney, haricot, snap, string, pole and butter beans. Chickpeas were mashed and baked in chili-flavored dishes, or eaten with hot sausages called *chorizo piquante.*

Settlers wrapped their food in *tortillas* and in *guayabes,* which were thin rolls of corn bread made by pouring corn meal onto a hot rock and rolling it up. *Gritted bread* was made by rubbing unripened corn kernels on perforated tin to form a moist meal that would bake like spoon-bread. Italian miners added their influence by providing spicy tomato sauce recipes.

In the Great Basin cold desert of Colorado and Utah, European settlers introduced new breads such as *pumpernickel* from Germany and dark rye and whole wheat breads from Scandinavia. German bock beer and ale were favorites in home breweries, and bread recipes using beer were brought to the kitchen.

*The secret to this recipe is to cut down through the center of the kernels (not between kernels) before scraping the cob so that the "milk" goes into the pudding.*

## CORN PUDDING

- 4 or 5 ears corn
- 3 egg yolks
- 2 tablespoons butter or margarine, melted
- 2 tablespoons sugar
- 1 teaspoon salt
- 2 cups milk
- 3 stiff-beaten egg whites

With sharp knife, make cuts down center of kernels on each row. Scrape cob. Measure 1¾ cups corn. Beat egg yolks till thick and lemon-colored. Stir in corn, butter or margarine, sugar and salt. Slowly beat in milk. Fold in egg whites. Pour into 8x8x2-inch baking dish; bake in 350° oven for 45 to 50 minutes. Makes 6 to 8 servings.

## SOURDOUGH PANCAKES

- 1 cup Sourdough Starter (recipe on page 75)
- 1 cup all-purpose flour
- 1 teaspoon sugar

# BURIED AT BOOT HILL

In the early cowtowns, where the chances of being killed in a shoot-out were high, many men died and were buried with their boots on.

Several cowtowns had a cemetery on a rise at the edge of town known as Boot Hill. The first Boot Hill was in Dodge City, Kansas.

This city was created by the Santa Fe Railroad and it quickly became the cattle center of the country and a transient cowboy's paradise. In 1876 the town had 1,200 inhabitants and 20 saloons. Frequent shoot-outs made a temporary cemetery a necessity in the lawless cowtown.

Dodge City's Boot Hill was simple in design. Wooden markers usually identified the booted corpses. Sometimes more elaborate markers had epitaphs burned into them. "Died of lead poisoning," meant the gun slinger died of a bullet wound, while a cattle rustler's epitaph read "Too many irons in the fire."

*Salads, Vegetables & Breads*

½ teaspoon baking soda
½ teaspoon salt
1 beaten egg
½ cup water
2 tablespoons shorten-
    ing or lard, melted

Bring Sourdough Starter to room temperature. In bowl stir together flour, sugar, baking soda and salt. Add Sourdough Starter, egg, water and shortening; mix well. For each pancake pour about ¼ cup batter onto a hot, lightly greased griddle or heavy skillet. Cook till golden brown, turning once. Serve hot with maple syrup. Makes 10 to 12 pancakes.

## CACTUS SALAD
*(pictured right)*

1 15-ounce jar (about
    2 cups) cactus in
    salt water, drained
    and cut into strips
1 4-ounce jar sliced
    pimiento, drained
    • • •
¼ cup *Coors* beer
2 tablespoons salad oil
1 tablespoon lemon
    juice
1 tablespoon thinly
    sliced green onion
1 clove garlic, minced
⅛ teaspoon pepper

Arrange cactus in 10x6x2-inch baking dish. Arrange pimiento over cactus. Combine Coors, oil, lemon juice, green onion, garlic and pepper; pour over cactus. Cover; chill 1 hour. Serves 4.

Cactus Salad

Cowboy Beans

## COWBOY BEANS

*(pictured left)*

- 1 **pound dry pinto beans**
- 1 **12-ounce can *Coors* beer**
- 1 **pound smoked ham hocks**
- ½ **cup chopped onion**
- 1 **16-ounce can tomatoes, cut up**
- 3 **tablespoons molasses**
- 1 **teaspoon dry mustard**
- ¼ **teaspoon pepper**

Rinse beans. Combine beans and 7 cups *water*. Bring to boiling. Simmer 2 minutes; remove from heat. Cover; let stand 1 hour. Drain.

Combine beans, Coors, and 2 cups *water*. Add ham hocks and onion; cover and simmer 1 hour, stirring occasionally. Remove ham hocks. Remove meat from bones; chop. Discard bones. Return meat to beans along with tomatoes, molasses, dry mustard and pepper. Cover and simmer 1 hour more or till beans are tender, stirring occasionally. Add additional water or Coors, if necessary. Makes 8 servings.

## APPLE FLAPJACKS

- 1 **beaten egg**
- 1 **cup milk**
- ¾ **cup *Coors* beer**
- ⅓ **cup cooking oil**
- 2 **cups packaged pancake mix**
- 1 **cup chopped apple or whole blackberries**

**Butter or margarine**
**Maple-flavored syrup**

In mixing bowl combine egg, milk, Coors and cooking oil. Place pancake mix in another mixing bowl. Add egg mixture; beat till smooth. Gently fold in desired fruit. Bake batter on hot, lightly greased griddle using ¼ *cup* batter for each pancake. Cook till golden, turning when pancakes have bubbly surface and slightly dry edges. If batter thickens while standing, add a little additional Coors or milk to desired consistency. Serve with butter and maple-flavored syrup. Makes 14 to 16 (4-inch) pancakes.

## BEER CORN BREAD

- 1 **cup yellow cornmeal**
- 1 **cup all-purpose flour**
- 2 **teaspoons baking powder**
- ¾ **teaspoon salt**
- ½ **teaspoon baking soda**
- 2 **beaten eggs**
- ½ **cup milk**
- ½ **cup *Coors* beer**
- ¼ **cup cooking oil**

In bowl stir together cornmeal, flour, baking powder, salt and soda. Combine eggs, milk, Coors and shortening; add to dry ingredients. Mix well. Turn into greased 8x8x2-inch baking pan. Bake in 425° oven for 15 minutes or till done. Serve warm with molasses or maple syrup, if desired. Makes 9 servings.

*Salads, Vegetables & Breads*

## INDIAN WILD RICE

- ½ cup wild rice
- ¾ cup *Coors* beer
- ¼ teaspoon salt
- 4 slices bacon
- 1 cup sliced fresh mushrooms
- 1 cup shredded carrot
- ½ cup chopped onion

Run cold water over rice in strainer for 1 minute, lifting rice to rinse well. In saucepan combine rice, Coors, salt and ½ cup *water*. Bring to boiling. Cover and simmer 40 to 50 minutes. Meanwhile, cook bacon till crisp; drain, reserving 2 tablespoons drippings. Crumble bacon and set aside. Cook mushrooms, carrot and onion in drippings till tender. Stir in rice; heat through. Turn into serving bowl; sprinkle with crumbled bacon. Serves 6.

## ORIGINAL GUACAMOLE

- 2 large avocados, peeled and seeded
- 2 large tomatoes, peeled, seeded and chopped
- 3 green onions
- 1 or 2 fresh serrano chili peppers, finely chopped
- 2 tablespoons snipped cilantro or parsley
- 2 tablespoons lime juice
- ¼ teaspoon salt
- 3 tomatillos (optional)
  Tortilla Chips

In mixing bowl mash the avocados till almost smooth.

Stir in chopped tomatoes, green onions, chili peppers, cilantro, lime juice, salt and the tomatillos, if desired. Cover and chill about 1 hour before serving. Serve with Tortilla Chips. Makes 2½ cups.

**Tortilla Chips:** Stack one 10-ounce package *corn tortillas* (12); cut into 6 pie-shaped wedges. In heavy frying pan heat 1½ inches of *cooking oil*. Fry the tortilla pieces, a few at a time, in hot oil (365°) about 1 minute or till golden. Drain chips well on paper toweling. Makes 72.

## MARINATED VEGETABLES

- 1 medium cucumber, thinly sliced
- 1 medium green pepper, cut into strips
- 1 cup broccoli buds
- 1 cup halved fresh mushrooms
- 1 cup cherry tomatoes
  • • •
- ½ cup *Coors* beer
- ¼ cup salad oil
- 2 tablespoons vinegar
- ¾ teaspoon dried basil, crushed
- ¾ teaspoon dillseed
- ½ teaspoon salt
  Dash pepper

In bowl combine vegetables. Combine Coors and remaining ingredients; pour over vegetables. Cover and chill at least 4 hours. Serves 8 to 10.

## SOURDOUGH FRENCH BREAD

- 1 package active dry yeast
- 1 12-ounce can *Coors* beer, warmed to 110°
- 5 to 5½ cups all-purpose flour
- 1 cup Coors Sourdough Starter at room temperature (recipe on page 75)
- 3 tablespoons sugar
- 2 tablespoons butter or margarine, softened
- 2 teaspoons salt
- ½ teaspoon baking soda
  Yellow cornmeal

Soften yeast in warm Coors. Blend in *2 cups* of the flour, the Sourdough Starter, sugar, butter and salt. Combine *1 cup* of the flour and the soda; stir into flour-yeast mixture. Stir in as much of the remaining flour as you can with a spoon. Knead in enough remaining flour to make a moderately stiff dough that is smooth and elastic (5 to 8 minutes total). Place in greased bowl; turn once. Cover; let rise till double, 1 to 1½ hours. Punch down; divide in half. Cover; let rest 10 minutes. Shape into 2 oblong or round loaves. Place on greased baking sheet sprinkled with cornmeal. Cover; let rise till almost double, about 1 hour. Brush with a little water. Make diagonal slashes across tops. Bake in 375° oven for 30 to 35 minutes. Makes 2 loaves.

*Salads, Vegetables & Breads*

# SOURDOUGH

The finest contribution a cook on the trail could make was his sourdough because it provided his rolling camp with fresh, tasty bread daily.

Flour and warm water with a little salt were mixed together and placed in a keg, which was then covered and put in a warm place to ferment for a day or two. Sometimes a handful of sugar, a little molasses or a piece of potato was added to speed up the fermentation.

Each day the keg was placed in the sun and each night it was wrapped in a blanket to keep the starter warm. Sometimes cooks were even known to take the keg to bed with them on cool nights.

When breadbaking time came, the cook would use only half the bubbly mixture in the keg, and to the rest he would add more flour, water and salt to replace what he took out. The bread was mixed and then kneaded on the floured work table at the back of the chuck wagon. Cowboys could usually tell when the cook had made fresh bread: His hands were clean from kneading the dough.

## SOURDOUGH STARTER

1 **package active dry yeast**
1 **cup warm water (110°)**
2 **cups all-purpose flour**
1 **12-ounce can** *Coors* **beer**
1 **tablespoon sugar**

Soften yeast in warm water. Stir in flour, Coors and sugar. Beat till smooth. Place in a wide-mouth jar. Cover loosely with cheesecloth; let stand at room temperature 5 to 10 days, stirring 2 to 3 times a day. Mixture will foam and bubble. (Time required to ferment depends on room temperature; if room is warm, let stand a shorter time than if room is cool.) Cover loosely and refrigerate till ready to use.

*To keep Starter going:* For each 1 cup Starter used, add ¾ cup *water*, ¾ cup *all-purpose flour*, and 1 teaspoon *sugar* to remainder. Let stand at room temperature till bubbly, at least a day. Cover loosely and refrigerate for later use. If not used within 10 days, add 1 teaspoon *sugar*. Repeat adding sugar every 10 days.

## BEER-GLAZED CARROTS

- 3 cups bias-sliced carrots*
- 2 slices bacon
- ½ cup chopped green pepper
- ¼ cup chopped onion
- 1 teaspoon cornstarch
- ⅓ cup *Coors* beer
- ½ teaspoon sugar
- ½ teaspoon dried basil, crushed
- ⅛ teaspoon salt
- ⅛ teaspoon dried rosemary, crushed
- 2 tablespoons snipped parsley

In covered saucepan cook carrots in small amount of boiling salted water 15 to 20 minutes or till crisp-tender; drain. Meanwhile, in skillet cook bacon till crisp. Remove bacon, reserving *1 tablespoon* drippings in skillet. Crumble bacon; set aside.

In the skillet cook green pepper and onion in reserved drippings till tender but not brown. Blend in cornstarch. Add Coors to skillet along with sugar, basil, salt and rosemary. Cook and stir till bubbly; cook and stir 1 minute more. Stir in cooked carrots; heat through. Sprinkle with crumbled bacon and parsley. Serve immediately. Makes 6 to 8 servings.

*Note: Substitute 1 pound fresh green beans, cut into 1-inch pieces (3 cups) for the carrots, if desired.

# HIGH COUNTRY COOKING

When flatlanders first started crossing the mountains of the West and tried out some of their favorite recipes, they had a few surprises in store for them — recipes that work at sea level often did not work at 10,000 feet. The reason: Higher altitudes have lower air pressure.

Yeast breads, quick breads and cakes are particularly affected by high altitudes. With less air pressure to control the leavening agent, breads rise too quickly and cakes fall. Because liquids boil at lower temperatures in high altitudes, evaporation occurs more rapidly causing drier baked products. As the liquid evaporates, the sugar becomes more concentrated. In cakes, this higher sugar concentration results in a weaker cell structure and causes cakes to fall.

It is generally agreed that most high-altitude baking problems occur over 2,500 feet. Although there is no magic formula for adapting recipes to high altitudes, there are some guidelines.

For each teaspoon of baking powder, soda or cream of tartar in a recipe, *reduce* it by ⅛ teaspoon at 3,000 feet, or by ¼ teaspoon at 7,000 feet. For each cup of liquid, *increase* it by 1 to 2 tablespoons at 3,000 feet, or by 3 to 4 tablespoons at 7,000 feet. And for each cup of sugar, *decrease* it by up to 1 tablespoon at 3,000 feet, or by 1 to 3 tablespoons at 7,000 feet.

For cakes and cookies, increase the oven temperature 15 to 20 degrees. This allows cake batters to "set" before the leavening agent expands too much, and cookies will not be as dry. Since yeast bread doughs also rise more quickly, resulting in a weaker structure, reduce the amount of yeast used or shorten the rising time.

*The Dutch, who traditionally gave a waffle iron to every Dutch bride, brought waffles to the American West. Denver's early Dutch community served delicious malt beer waffles topped with shredded lemon peel and powdered sugar.*

## DUTCH MALT BEER WAFFLES

- 1 cup all-purpose flour
- ⅓ cup instant malted milk powder (plain flavor)
- 2½ teaspoons baking powder
- ¼ teaspoon salt
- 2 egg yolks
- ⅔ cup *Coors* beer
- ¼ cup butter or margarine, melted
- 2 egg whites
  Butter or margarine
  Maple-flavored syrup

In large mixing bowl stir together the flour, instant malted milk powder, baking powder and salt till thoroughly combined. In another mixing bowl beat the egg yolks with a fork. Gradually beat in Coors and the melted butter.

In mixer bowl beat the egg whites with an electric mixer on high speed till stiff peaks form. Stir the beer mixture into the dry ingredients. Gently fold in the egg whites.

Carefully pour some batter onto the grids of preheated, lightly greased waffle baker. Close the lid; bake for 3 to 4 minutes or till waffle is done. *Do not open lid during baking.*

Use a fork to help lift the baked waffle off grid. Repeat with remaining batter. To keep baked waffles hot for serving, place in a warm oven. Serve with butter and maple-flavored syrup. Makes six 7-inch waffles.

## BACON-STUFFED SQUASH

- 6 small patty pan squash
- 6 slices bacon
- ⅓ cup chopped onion
- ⅓ cup chopped celery
- ½ cup herb-seasoned stuffing mix

Cook squash, covered, in boiling salted water for about 15 minutes or till tender. Drain; cool. To make squash cups, cut a small slice from stem end. Scoop out the center of each squash, leaving ½-inch rim at edge. Finely chop squash from center and tops; set aside. Sprinkle squash cups with a little salt. Cook bacon till crisp. Drain; reserving 2 tablespoons of the drippings. Crumble bacon; set aside. Cook the onion and celery in the reserved drippings till tender. Stir in stuffing mix, the reserved chopped squash and crumbled bacon. Fill squash cups. Place in 10x6x2-inch baking dish; cover. Bake in 350° oven for about 30 minutes. Makes 6 servings.

 *Sour milk can be made by adding 1 tablespoon lemon juice or vinegar to 1 cup of milk. Wait 5 minutes for it to "sour."*

## SOUR MILK BISCUITS

- 2 cups all-purpose flour
- 1 tablespoon baking powder
- ½ teaspoon salt
- ¼ teaspoon baking soda
- ⅓ cup lard or shortening
- ¾ cup sour milk

In mixing bowl stir together flour, baking powder, salt and soda. Cut in lard or shortening till mixture resembles coarse crumbs. Stir in milk just till dry ingredients are moistened. Knead on lightly floured surface 10 to 12 times. Roll out or pat to ½-inch thickness. Cut into 2½-inch rounds. Place on ungreased baking sheet. Bake in 450° oven for 10 to 12 minutes. Makes 12 biscuits.

## PIONEER SALAD DRESSING

- 1 cup whipping cream
- 2 tablespoons sugar
- ¼ teaspoon salt
- ¼ cup vinegar

Whip cream with sugar and salt till mixture begins to thicken; stir in vinegar. Toss with salad greens. Makes about 1½ cups.

Salads, Vegetables & Breads

## DANDELION GREEN SALAD

- 4 cups young, tender dandelion greens or other greens
- 2 hard-cooked eggs, chopped
- 4 slices bacon, cut up
- ⅓ cup *Coors* beer
- 1 tablespoon honey

In salad bowl combine dandelion greens and chopped eggs; set aside. In skillet cook bacon till crisp. Remove from heat. Stir Coors and honey into bacon and drippings. Pour over salad; toss to coat. Makes 4 servings.

 *This hot pasta dish originated with the Chihuahuan mule drivers who used the Camino Real (Royal Road) from Mexico City to El Paso.*

## SPAGHETTI AL MOJO ARRIERO

- 1 pound spaghetti
- 4 cloves garlic, minced
- 2 tablespoons cooking oil
- 2 tablespoons olive oil
- 2 cups shredded Muenster cheese (8 ounces)
- 3 fresh serrano or jalapeño peppers, finely chopped
- 2 tablespoons snipped cilantro or parsley

In Dutch oven cook spaghetti in large amount of boiling salted water till tender; drain well. Return to Dutch oven.

Meanwhile, in small skillet cook garlic in the cooking oil and olive oil till garlic is golden. Add garlic mixture and shredded cheese to hot cooked spaghetti; toss well to mix.

Transfer hot spaghetti mixture to a serving platter and top with chili peppers and cilantro. Sprinkle with *salt* and *pepper*. Toss lightly to mix; serve immediately. Serves 8.

## COORS BREAD

*(pictured right)*

- 3 cups all-purpose flour
- 1 tablespoon baking powder
- 1 tablespoon sugar
- ½ teaspoon baking soda
- 2 eggs, beaten
- 1 cup *Coors* beer
- ½ cup water
- ⅓ cup cooking oil

Combine flour, baking powder, sugar, baking soda and 1 teaspoon *salt*. Set aside 1 tablespoon of the beaten egg. Combine remaining egg, Coors, water and oil; add to dry ingredients all at once, stirring just till moistened (batter will be slightly lumpy). Pour into a greased 8x4x3-inch loaf pan. Brush top with reserved 1 tablespoon egg. Bake in a 350° oven for 60 minutes or until wooden pick inserted near center comes out clean. Remove from pan; cool on wire rack. Makes 1 loaf.

*Salads, Vegetables & Breads*

**Coors Bread**

Coastlines

*P*erhaps more than mountain, desert, prairie or river, the great Pacific coastline represented new life to travelers from Asia who crossed the ocean, and those from the East who arrived by foot and wagon. The coast was a beginning— a rebirth for lives that had foundered elsewhere; it was an end to an arduous journey, the destination of many dreams.

> "The shattered water
> made a misty din,
> Great waves looked over others
> coming in,
> And thought of doing
> something to the shore
> That water never did to land
> before . . .
> It looked as if a night of
> dark intent
> Was coming, and not only a
> night, an age.

— From "Once By The Pacific" from *The Poetry of Robert Frost*

## Missions and Miners

The early pioneers who traveled the Oregon and Santa Fe trails were not the first to see roaring waves and hear the whisper of redwoods and fir trees. The coastline had been inhabited by Indians and by the Spanish padres who tried to convert them to Christianity. It may have been the padres' need for Communion wine that gave rise to the first California vineyards.

Citrus fruit trees, dates and figs were brought from Spain by explorers eager to test the potential of the new land. Salmon and sturgeon, which had fed generations of Indian families, now fed the new settlers.

Indians on the lush, green northwest coast had developed rich traditions which later were mimicked by the white man. The ceremonial *potlatch,* a ritual designed to demonstrate social status, was a lavish series of feasts and gift giving that could be prompted by a birth, a wedding or the passing of property to family heirs.

When the California gold rush of 1849 lured swarms of Easterners and immigrants from Europe and Asia, the land was not equipped to feed such numbers. Early miners ate a diet of corn, beans and beef with a few "imports" such as flour which was often filled with worms by the time it reached the coast.

Settlers in the Pacific Northwest were lumberjacks, miners, farmers and fishermen. They learned from the Indians to eat indigenous foods such as the wild *camas lily,* which resembled an onion and was sweet when cooked.

This spartan life began to change when settlers adapted to the warm climate of the southern and central coast, and exploited the rich soil. Norwegian and Portuguese fishermen applied their skills to the Pacific, and found it a rich source of tuna, Dungeness crab, tiny grunion and schools of anchovies.

Menus expanded and American settlers experimented with seasoning and serving techniques, learning from their Italian and Greek neighbors, in particular, that meals could be explosions of flavor, color and celebration.

## The Age of Experimentation

Perhaps because they were inspired by the diversity of foods available from both land and sea, coastal settlers took to expanding their diets and their eating places. Lavish restaurants and saloons flourished in San Francisco, an international city which quickly became known for fine food.

Chefs came from France to take advantage of the bounty of vegetables, fruits and seafoods. Restaurants such as Lazzuro's and Kinkand's catered to new communities of European immigrants and growing cosmopolitan tastes. At the Occidental Hotel in San Francisco, the famous bartender Jerry Thomas created a world of new drink concoctions and published the popular *Bon Vivant's Companion* guide to good living.

The coast stimulated a new trend in food and drink in the West. Newly arrived cooks altered the character of American cakes by introducing ingredients such as cream of tartar, baking powder and beer which was used to lighten batters. Immigrants from the Austro-Hungarian empire supposedly never had a dessertless meal, no matter how poor they were. Cake and cookie sales became tools to raise

# COFFEE AND TEA

America's affinity for coffee dates back to the Boston Tea Party in Revolutionary days when it became unpatriotic to drink tea. Never was this fondness more apparent than in the West where tired, thirsty cowboys drank strong, harsh coffee morning, noon and night. No milk or sugar softened the blow of Arbuckles "six-shooter" coffee.

Arbuckles, perhaps the most popular coffee in the West, came as roasted beans which had to be ground before brewing. Cleverly, the beans were coated with egg whites and sugar to preserve their flavor.

In 1875, Arbuckles offered a peppermint stick as a premium. On cattle drives, cooks would yell "who wants to grind" (the Arbuckles), and the cowboys would come running. The grinder got a peppermint stick as his reward.

Campfire coffee was made by mixing an egg yolk, or a combination of yolk, white and shell, with the coffee grounds before brewing. This practice added flavor and cleared murky coffee. If eggs were unavailable, a fish skin was substituted.

A West Coast drink that substituted for coffee was green tea which was most frequently enjoyed by poor folks. *Slumgullion* was Mark Twain's name for an almost-tea concoction which served in place of tea. Tea substitutes in the early West included mint leaves, marjoram, chamomile, sage and marigold leaves.

money, and American desserts entered the growing world of competitive achievement.

Beverage availability increased with the introduction of refrigerated rail cars late in the 19th Century, and with new products such as canned milk, Story has it that cowboys did not like canned milk, even though they could have used it for parched throats on the range. When one milk company offered a prize for a winning canned milk advertising slogan, a pioneer woman wrote:

> Carnation milk, best in the
>    land,
> Comes to the table in a
>    little red can.

She passed her entry along to a cowboy to take it into town to be mailed, then waited for weeks before she heard that her entry was unacceptable. When she related the story to the cowboy, he sheepishly confessed that he had made a few improvements so that the slogan read:

> Carnation milk, best in the
>    land,
> Comes to the table in a
>    little red can.
> No teats to pull, no hay to
>    pitch,
> Just punch a hole in the
>    s _ _ _ _ _ _ _ _ _ h!

— From *Come An' Get It: The Story of The Old Cowboy Cook* by Ramon F. Adams. Copyright 1952 by University of Oklahoma Press.

No doubt the literary cowpoke incurred the woman's wrath with his poetic license.

# DRIED DINNER

Hunters, trappers and prospectors moving west had to carry their own food, and dried foods were the easiest to pack and eat on the trail.

The West's arid climate and bright sunshine provided ideal conditions for drying food and keeping it edible indefinitely.

Dried meats such as jerky and pemmican provided concentrated, lightweight foods for quick energy and tasty meals. Jerky was made of thin strips of beef, venison or buffalo that were highly seasoned and sun dried. It could be eaten as a snack or added to stews.

Pemmican, a staple of Indians, was formed into square chunks and stashed in caches along trails to provide food for future trips. It was made of dried meat pounded into powder with meat fat and wild berries added.

 *After the Pueblo Indians were introduced to Catholicism, the Feast Day of St. John the Baptist became one of their time-honored celebrations. These cookies, rolled out and shaped into special designs, are always included in the ceremonies.*

## INDIAN FEAST DAY COOKIES

| | |
|---|---|
| 1½ | cups sugar |
| 1 | cup shortening |
| 1 | beaten egg |
| ¼ | cup milk |
| 1 | teaspoon vanilla |
| 2 | cups all-purpose flour |
| 1 | cup whole wheat flour |
| ½ | cup finely chopped pine nuts |
| 1 | teaspoon baking powder |
| ¼ | teaspoon salt |

Beat together sugar and shortening till light and fluffy. Combine egg, milk and vanilla. Stir together flours, pine nuts, baking powder and salt; add to creamed mixture alternately with liquid, beating well after each. On lightly floured surface roll half of the dough at a time to a 12x6-inch rectangle. Cut into eighteen 2-inch squares. Make ¾-inch cuts about ½ inch apart into each side of the cookie.

*Beverages, Snacks & Desserts*

Gently lift sections apart, making a two-sided fan shape. Place on ungreased cookie sheet. Bake in 350° oven for 15 to 16 minutes. Remove from cookie sheet; cool on rack. Makes 3 dozen cookies.

## CHILI CON QUESO
*(pictured right)*

½ cup chopped onion
1 tablespoon butter or margarine
1 4-ounce can chopped green chilies, drained
1 medium tomato, peeled, seeded and finely chopped
¼ teaspoon salt
¾ cup *Coors* beer
Dash bottled hot pepper sauce
1½ cups shredded Monterey Jack cheese
1 cup shredded cheddar cheese
4 teaspoons cornstarch
Tortilla chips

Cook onion in butter till tender. Stir in chilies, tomato and salt. Add Coors and the bottled hot pepper sauce. Simmer, uncovered, for 10 minutes. Combine cheeses and cornstarch; stir into chili mixture, a little at a time, till cheese is melted. Serve immediately with tortilla chips. Keep warm in fondue pot over low heat. (Add a little additional warm Coors if mixture thickens.) Makes 2½ cups.

Chili con Queso

**Stack Cake**

 *Stack Cake was a traditional pioneer wedding cake that was put together right at the wedding. Each guest brought a layer of cake. Applesauce was spread between layers, and all the layers were stacked. A bride's popularity could be measured by the number of layers she received. This simple molasses cake was typical.*

## STACK CAKE
*(pictured left)*

- 1 cup butter
- 1 cup sugar
- 1 cup molasses
- 3 eggs
- 4 cups all-purpose flour
- 1 teaspoon baking soda
- 1 teaspoon salt
- 1 cup *Coors* beer
- 2 15-ounce jars chunk-style applesauce
- ½ teaspoon ground cinnamon
  Whipped cream
  Sliced apples

Grease and flour three 8x1½-inch round baking pans; set aside. In large mixing bowl cream butter and sugar till light and fluffy. Beat in molasses; add eggs, one at a time, beating well after each. Stir together flour, baking soda and salt; add to creamed mixture alternately with Coors, beating after each addition. Pour 1⅓ cups batter into each prepared pan. (Refrigerate remaining batter.) Bake in 375° oven about 15 minutes or till cake tests done. Cool in pans 5 minutes; remove from pans and cool on wire racks. Wash pans; grease and flour. Repeat baking with remaining batter. Combine applesauce and cinnamon; spread between cooled cake layers. Spread whipped cream on top; garnish with sliced apples. Serve with additional whipped cream. Makes 20 to 24

## MEXICAN HOT SAUSAGE DIP

- ½ pound bulk Italian pork sausage
- 1 15-ounce can pinto beans, drained and mashed
- 1 cup shredded sharp cheddar cheese
- ½ cup *Coors* beer
- 1 or 2 serrano chili peppers, thinly sliced
- ½ teaspoon dried oregano, crushed
- ⅛ teaspoon garlic powder
  Taco shells, broken or tortilla chips

In 2-quart saucepan cook sausage 15 minutes or till browned; drain fat. Add beans, cheese, Coors, chili peppers, oregano and garlic powder. Heat through. Transfer mixture to electric cooking pot or fondue pot, adding more Coors, if necessary, to make a good dipping consistency. Serve with broken taco shells. Makes 2¼ cups dip.

*Beverages, Snacks & Desserts*

# BEAN-SAUSAGE TERRINE WITH GOAT CHEESE

- 1 **pound dried pinto beans**
- 2 **cups** *Coors* **beer**
- 2 **cloves garlic**
- 1 **teaspoon dried oregano, crushed**
- 1½ **pounds bulk Italian pork sausage**
- ½ **pound finely chopped fresh pork**
- ¼ **pound smoked bacon, diced**
- 4 **pasilla or ancho chili peppers, chopped**
- ½ **teaspoon bottled hot pepper sauce**
- 6 **to 8 ounces goat cheese, sliced**
  **Pico de Gallo Salsa (see recipe, page 31)**
  **Crackers or bread slices**

Soak beans overnight in enough water to cover. (*Or*, in large saucepan combine beans and 6 cups *water*. Bring to boiling; boil 3 minutes. Cover and let stand 1 hour.) Drain and rinse beans; place in large saucepan. Stir in Coors, garlic, oregano and 4 cups *water*. Bring to boiling; reduce heat. Simmer, covered, 3 hours or till beans are very tender. Drain.

Remove *three-fourths* of beans. Place half at a time in food processor or blender container and process till smooth. Reserve remaining whole cooked beans.

In large skillet cook sausage, chopped pork and bacon over medium heat for 15 minutes or till well done. *Do not drain.* Stir in mashed beans; cook till quite thick. Stir in reserved whole beans, chili peppers, hot pepper sauce and 1 teaspoon *salt*. Turn *half* the mixture into 9x5x3-inch loaf pan lined with plastic wrap. Press sliced goat cheese into center; top with remaining bean mixture. Press lightly. Cover and chill 6 hours or overnight.

To serve, unmold and slice. Serve with Pico de Gallo Salsa and crackers.

 *This lemon custard pie originated in England as a lemon curd, or cheese (chess), tart. Today Chess Pie, a lemony egg-butter mixture, is especially popular in Texas.*

# CHESS PIE

  **Pastry for single-crust 9-inch pie**
- 1½ **cups sugar**
- 3 **tablespoons butter or margarine, melted**
- 1 **tablespoon all-purpose flour**
- 1 **tablespoon cornmeal**
- ½ **teaspoon vanilla**
- 1 **teaspoon finely shredded lemon peel**
- 5 **lightly beaten eggs**
- ¾ **cup milk**

Prepare and roll out pastry. Line 9-inch pie plate. Trim pastry to ½ inch beyond edge of pie plate. Flute edge; *do not prick pastry*. Line with heavyduty foil. Bake in 450° oven for 5 minutes. Remove foil. Cool.

For filling, in bowl combine sugar, butter, flour, cornmeal, vanilla and lemon peel. Stir in eggs and milk; mix well. Place pastry shell on oven rack. Pour filling into pastry shell. To prevent overbrowning, cover edge of pie with foil. Bake in 350° oven 20 minutes. Remove foil and bake 20 to 25 minutes more or till a knife inserted near center comes out clean. Cool on wire rack. Cover and chill to store. Makes one 9-inch pie.

# TAVERN CHEESE SPREAD

- 2 **cups finely shredded cheddar cheese at room temperature**
- 2 **tablespoons butter or margarine, softened**
- 1 **teaspoon prepared mustard**
- ½ **teaspoon prepared horseradish**
- ¼ **teaspoon pepper**
- ½ **cup** *Coors* **beer**

In blender container combine cheese, butter, mustard, horseradish and pepper. Heat Coors just to boiling; pour over cheese. Blend till smooth. Spoon into bowl. Cover and chill. Let stand at room temperature about 1 hour before serving. Makes 1 cup.

*Beverages, Snacks & Desserts*

# SERVING BEER

Because beer is such a versatile beverage, pouring and serving methods are often best left to the drinker.

Bill Coors says beer should be served any way you like it. "But many people enjoy it as cold as you can get it," he says.

For parties, Bill usually serves his beer in cans or bottles placed in large bowls of ice. He prefers to pour his beer "as gently as possible down the side of a glass so that it retains as much of its carbonation as possible." Bill also recommends Coors or Coors Light on the rocks. "But make sure they are wet rocks (ice rinsed in water) so that the beer does not become flat while you're drinking it," he says.

Another important element in pouring a good beer is the glasses. The least trace of soap film, grease or lint will flatten the beer. Glasses should be washed in dishwater with detergent, not soap. Baking soda or salt may be added to the wash water instead of detergent.

Always rinse in clean water and air dry. Do not towel dry.

To order beer for a party, consider the following: In warm weather, the average person may drink a 12-ounce container of beer every half hour. For a party of 12 to 18 people buy 4 cases of beer, for 25 to 30 people buy 8 cases and for 36 to 42 you'll need 12 cases.

When combined with other ingredients beer makes excellent cocktails.

## FUN AND FOAMY BEER COCKTAILS

**Shandygaff:** Fill a tall glass with half *Coors* and half *ginger ale.*

**Black Velvet:** Fill tall glass with half *Coors* and half *champagne.*

**Red Beer:** Fill tall glass with half *Coors* and half *tomato juice.*

**Indibeer:** Fill tall glass with half *Coors* and half *orange juice;* season with a little *curry powder.*

**Boilermaker:** Serve a jigger of *rye whiskey* alongside a cold, tall glass of *Coors.*

**Beer Buster:** Add a jigger of *gin* or *vodka* to a cold, tall glass of *Coors.* Add a dash or two of bottled *hot pepper sauce.*

**Cup of Gold:** Spike a cold, tall glass of *Coors* with a jigger of *gin* or *vodka,* a jigger of *lime juice,* and a little *superfine sugar.*

**Bloody Bull in Ice:** Combine 3 cups *tomato juice,* 2 teaspoons *Worcestershire sauce,* and several dashes bottled *hot pepper sauce;* pour into ice cube tray. Place a quartered *lemon slice* into each cube section of tray. Freeze. To serve, fill tall glass with frozen cubes; pour in *Coors* to fill glass.

**Lager and Lime:** Stir 1 to 2 tablespoons *lime juice* into a cold, tall glass of *Coors.*

*Army cooks made this pie when no fresh or dried apples were available. The recipe was discovered at Ft. Robinson, Nebraska, a historic cavalry post.*

## MOCK APPLE PIE

> Pastry for double-crust
> 9-inch pie
> 2 eggs
> 25 saltine crackers,
> broken (about 1½
> cups)
> 1½ cups milk
> 1 cup sugar
> 2 teaspoons ground
> cinnamon
> 1 teaspoon finely
> shredded lemon peel
> ½ teaspoon ground
> nutmeg
> Vanilla ice cream or
> light cream (optional)

Prepare and roll out pastry. Line 9-inch pie plate with half of pastry. Trim pastry to edge of plate. In large bowl beat eggs with fork. Stir in crackers, milk, sugar, cinnamon, lemon peel and nutmeg. Turn into pastry-lined pie plate.

Cut slits in top crust; place atop filling. Seal and flute edge. Brush with *milk* and sprinkle with *sugar*. To prevent overbrowning, cover edge of pie with foil. Bake in 375° oven 20 minutes. Remove foil; bake 25 to 30 minutes more or till crust is golden. Serve warm with ice cream, if desired. Makes one 9-inch pie.

# BEER TYPES

America's favorite type of beer is light lager, also called *Pilsner.* This is a tangy, pale-gold brew with 3 to 3.9 percent alcohol content by weight. Coors Premium is a Pilsner with a 3.6 percent alcohol content.

Other beer favorites include:

*Light beer*—contains fewer calories than Pilsner. Coors Light has 104 calories per 12-oz. serving compared to an average of 155 calories for Pilsners. Alcohol content of Coors Light is 3.3 percent.

*Ales*—dark, full-bodied brews with an alcohol content ranging from 4 to 5 percent.

*Porter and Stout*—darker, fuller-bodied ales with alcohol contents as high as 6.5 percent.

*Bock Beer*—heavy, dark lager, sweeter than most beer. Its alcohol content may be as high as 10 percent.

*Malt liquor*—a brew made with barley malt, similar to beer, but with an alcohol content over 5 percent.

*White beer*—brewed from wheat, barley malt and fruit syrup.

*Sake*—Japanese beverage brewed with rice instead of barley. It contains no carbonation and has a 14 to 16 percent alcohol content.

## BEER FRUITCAKE

- 2 12-ounce cans  beer
- 2 cups raisins
- 1 8-ounce package pitted dates, snipped
- 1 cup dried apples, chopped
- 1 cup dried apricots, chopped
- 4 cups all-purpose flour
- 1½ cups packed brown sugar
- 2 teaspoons pumpkin pie spice
- 1 teaspoon baking soda
- 1¼ cups butter
- 4 eggs
- 1 teaspoon shredded lemon peel
- 1 cup chopped walnuts

Pour *one can* of the Coors into saucepan; heat to boiling. Remove from heat. Add fruit; let stand 1 hour, stirring occasionally. Stir together flour, brown sugar, pumpkin pie spice and baking soda. Cut in butter till mixture resembles small peas. Combine eggs, the remaining can of Coors, and lemon peel; add to flour mixture, stirring well. Drain fruit mixture, reserving marinade. Fold fruit mixture and nuts into batter. Turn into greased and floured 10-inch tube pan. Bake in 300° oven about 2 hours or till cake tests done. Cool in pan on rack 10 minutes. Remove from pan; cool completely. Wrap in cheesecloth soaked in the reserved marinade, adding additional Coors, if necessary. Wrap tightly in foil. Store cake in cool place for up to 1 week before serving, remoistening cheesecloth with additional Coors as needed. Serves 24.

*This pudding was originally boiled in a cloth sack. Perhaps it got its name because it was so much trouble to make.*

## SON-OF-A-GUN-IN-A-SACK

- ¼ cup  beer
- 1 cup raisins
- 2¼ cups all-purpose flour
- ½ cup packed brown sugar
- 1 tablespoon baking soda
- 1 teaspoon salt
- 1 cup ground suet
- ⅔ cup Coors beer
- ½ cup chopped nuts
- ½ cup light molasses
  Whipped cream

Heat the ¼ cup Coors just to boiling; remove from heat and stir in raisins. Cover and let stand for 5 minutes. Combine flour, brown sugar, soda and salt. Stir in suet. Stir in undrained raisins, the remaining ⅔ cup Coors, the nuts and molasses; mix well. Arrange layers of cheesecloth to form a 16-inch square about ⅛ inch thick; set into a 1½-quart bowl. Fill cheesecloth-lined bowl with pudding mixture; bring up sides of cheesecloth, allowing room for expansion. Tie tightly. Place sack in large kettle or Dutch oven with boiling water to nearly cover. Cover; boil gently for 1¼ to 1½ hours or till pudding is done. Remove from boiling water; cool for 10 minutes. Unwrap pudding; invert onto wire rack to cool. Let stand 30 minutes. Serve warm with whipped cream. Serves 10 to 12.

*This flannel-smooth belly warmer is an early American hot drink that was served to the teamsters of wagon trains and stage lines. It tastes best with Coors' George Killian's Irish Red Ale®.*

## YARD OF FLANNEL

- 4 eggs
- ¼ cup sugar
- ¼ teaspoon ground ginger or nutmeg
- 1 quart George Killian's Irish Red Ale®
- ½ cup dark rum

In large nonmetal bowl beat together eggs, sugar and spice till thoroughly blended. In medium saucepan heat Killian's to almost boiling; remove from heat. Stir in rum. Gradually pour hot beer mixture into egg mixture, stirring constantly. Pour beer mixture back and forth between pan and bowl until the mixture is smooth and silky like flannel. Serve immediately. Makes 5 cups.

*Beverages, Snacks & Desserts*

## COORS CHEESECAKE

- ¾ cup all-purpose flour
- 3 tablespoons sugar
- 1½ teaspoons shredded lemon peel
- 6 tablespoons butter
- 3 egg yolks
- ¼ teaspoon vanilla
- 3 8-ounce packages cream cheese, softened
- 1½ cups shredded cheddar cheese, at room temperature
- 1¼ cups sugar
- 2 tablespoons cornstarch
- 2 teaspoons shredded orange peel
- 3 eggs
- ⅔ cup milk
- ¼ cup *Coors* beer

Combine flour, the 3 tablespoons sugar, and ½ *teaspoon* of the lemon peel. Cut in butter. Stir in *1* of the egg yolks, beaten, and vanilla. Pat two-thirds of the dough onto bottom of 9-inch springform pan (sides removed). Bake in 400° oven for 8 to 9 minutes or till golden; cool. Butter sides of pan; attach to bottom. Pat remaining dough onto sides of pan to a height of 1¾ inches. Increase oven temperature to 450°. Beat cream cheese till creamy. Add cheddar; beat about 10 minutes or till no yellow specks are visible. Combine the 1¼ cups sugar and cornstarch. Add to cheese along with orange peel and remaining 1 teaspoon lemon peel; mix well. Add eggs and remaining 2 egg yolks; mix just till blended. Stir in milk and Coors. Pour mixture into prepared pan. Bake in 450° oven for 10 minutes. Reduce oven to 300°; bake 55 to 60 minutes more or till center appears set. Remove from oven; cool 15 minutes. Loosen sides of cheesecake from pan with spatula. Cool 30 minutes; remove sides of pan. Cool 2 hours. Makes 12 servings.

## VINEGAR PIE

*(pictured right)*

- 1½ cups sugar
- 3 tablespoons cornstarch
- 3 tablespoons all-purpose flour
- 3 beaten egg yolks
- 2 tablespoons butter
- 3 to 4 tablespoons vinegar
- 1 9-inch baked pie shell Meringue

Combine sugar, cornstarch and flour. Stir in 1½ cups *water*. Cook and stir till mixture boils. Reduce heat; cook and stir 2 minutes more. Remove from heat. Gradually stir about 1 cup hot mixture into egg yolks; return all to saucepan. Cook and stir 2 minutes more. Stir in butter. Gradually stir in vinegar. Pour into pastry shell.

*Meringue:* In mixer bowl beat 3 *egg whites*, ½ teaspoon *vanilla* and ¼ teaspoon *cream of tartar* till soft peaks form. Gradually add 6 tablespoons *sugar*, beating to stiff peaks. Spread meringue over *hot* filling, sealing to pastry. Bake in 350° oven for 12 to 15 minutes. Cool; chill. Makes 1 pie.

## WHITE SUGAR GINGERBREAD

- 2 cups all-purpose flour
- 1 teaspoon baking powder
- 1 teaspoon ground ginger
- ½ teaspoon salt
- ½ teaspoon baking soda
- ¼ teaspoon ground nutmeg
- ½ cup butter or margarine
- 1 cup sugar
- 2 eggs
- 1 cup buttermilk Vanilla ice cream, whipped cream or fresh fruit (optional)

Grease and lightly flour 9x9x2-inch baking pan; set aside. In mixing bowl combine flour, baking powder, ginger, salt, baking soda and nutmeg; set flour mixture aside.

In large mixer bowl beat butter with electric mixer about 30 seconds. Add sugar and beat till well combined. Add eggs, one at a time, beating till fluffy. Add flour mixture and buttermilk alternately to beaten mixture, beating on low speed after each addition till just combined. Turn batter into prepared pan. Bake in 350° oven 35 to 40 minutes or till done. Cut into squares. Serve warm with ice cream, if desired. Makes 9 servings.

*Beverages, Snacks & Desserts*

Vinegar Pie

# RECIPES

# ACKNOWLEDGEMENTS

A good book, like a tasty recipe, is a combination of ingredients blended in just the right proportions. *Coors® Taste of the West* is the result of various creative ingredients provided by several persons, each of whom added their own bit of spice. A hearty thank you to all those who were involved in one way or another in the creation of this book, especially Bill Coors for providing copious information on everything from Coors family history to the proper way to serve beer; the late John McCarty for his unflagging determination and sponsorship of this project; Marj Hoobler and Nancy Newman for poring over copy and recipes to make sure everything was perfect; Gary Kelley for the beautifully distinctive drawings on the cover and interior; Tim Girvin for the distinctive and inimitable calligraphy; George de Gennaro for the food photography; Mable Hoffman and Patricia Winters for food styling; and Perry Struse, Jr. for landscape photography.

We gratefully acknowledge the following publishers and authors for permission to reprint their works:

From "Once By The Pacific" from *The Poetry of Robert Frost* edited by Edward Connery Lathem. Copyright 1928, ©1969 by Holt, Rinehart and Winston. Copyright ©1956 by Robert Frost. Reprinted by permission of Holt, Rinehart and Winston, Publishers.

From *The Prescott Courier*, Prescott, Arizona.

In "Women on the American Frontier" by Glenda Riley, in THE AMERICAN WEST ©1980 by Forum Press. Used by permission of the publisher.

From the book *In Grandmother's Day: A Legacy of Recipes, Remedies, and Country Wisdom from 100 Years Ago*, by Jean Cross. Copyright ©1980 by Jean Cross. Published by Prentice-Hall, Inc., Inglewood Cliffs, N.J. 07632.

From *Come An' Get It: The Story of The Old Cowboy Cook* by Ramon F. Adams. Copyright 1952 by University of Oklahoma Press.

From *A Dictionary of the Old West 1850-1900* by Peter Watts. Copyright ©1977 by Peter Watts. Reprinted by permission of Alfred A. Knopf, Inc.

From *Wild and Woolly* by Denis McLoughlin. Copyright ©1975 by Denis McLoughlin. Reprinted by permission of Doubleday & Company, Inc.